The Imaginary Poets

The
Imaginary Poets

Edited by Alan Michael Parker

TUPELO PRESS

First paperback edition November 2005
Library of Congress Control Number 2005903062

Tupelo Press
PO Box 539, Dorset, Vermont 05251
802.366.8185 • Fax 802.362.1883
editor@tupelopress.org • web www.tupelopress.org

Cover and text designed by William Kuch, WK Graphic Design

Acknowledgments

Thom Ward's section on the poet Jan DeKeerk was first published in *Salt Hill 15,*
Winter 2004 Issue, Syracuse University

Mark Strand's section on the poet Martin K was first published in *Tin House,*
vol 5, Spring 2004

Special thanks to Sally Dawidoff and Tina Chang.

*Tupelo Press is an award-winning independent literary press that
publishes fine fiction, non-fiction and poetry in books that are as much a joy
to hold as they are to read.*

*Tupelo Press is a registered 501(c)3 non-profit organization and relies on
donations to carry out its mission of publishing extraordinary work that may
be outside the realm of the large commercial publisher.*

Table of Contents

vii   *Introduction*

1   Aliki Barnstone as *Eva Victoria Perera*

9   Josh Bell as *Saurah Joan Mao*

21   Laure-Anne Bosselaar as *Anne-Maëlle Mathieu*

29   Martha Collins as *Hội An*

33   Annie Finch as *Rose Elbow Souris*

41   Judith Hall as *J II*

47   Barbara Hamby as *Gertrude of Brandenburg*

51   Jennifer Michael Hecht as *Kisaru Gashe*

55   Garrett Hongo as *Casey Shigemitsu*

61   Andrew Hudgins as *Alan Lutiy*

67   David Kirby as *Kevnor*

75   Maxine Kumin as *Greta Schoenemann-Licht*

81   Khaled Mattawa as *Tafida Zeinhum*

87   D.A. Powell as *João Pudim*

93   Kevin Prufer as *Wen Bo*

99   Anna Rabinowitz as *Hekenus*

107   Victoria Redel as *Tzadie Rackel*

113   David St. John as *Jean-Phillipe Dariens*

119   Mark Strand as *Marin K.*

127   Thom Ward as *Jan DeKeerk*

135   Rosanna Warren as *Anne Verveine*

141   Eleanor Wilner as *Irena Zupanik*

145   *Contributors' Biographies*

The Imaginary Poets

TRANSLATE A POEM into English, offer a biography of the poet, and then write a short essay in which the poem, the poet, and the corpus are considered—and make all of it up, without once indicating you have done so. Thus charged were the twenty-two contributors to this volume, who in response produced poems "translated" from eighteen languages including Dirja, Vietnamese, Yiddish, and even from Egyptian hieroglyphs, poems that may be read in the grand literary tradition of heteronyms and alter egos. Calling into question the axioms of translation and the use of fiction-in-poetry, the work that follows allows the contributors to slip between speaker, self, and other. I invite you to do likewise: read these poems aloud, speaker, self, and other.

Writing as someone else seems fundamental to what writers do. That a fiction writer invents his or her characters could even be a commonplace, notwithstanding such moments when a character in a work of fiction leads us to believe that he or she might be some version of the author, as in Jorge Luis Borges's "Borges and I" or Tim O'Brien's *The Things They Carried*. The poet as dramatic monologist seems a familiar pose as well, as can be seen in the poems of Robert Browning, C.P. Cavafy, and Robert Frost, or in the work of contemporary writers such as Ai and Carol Ann Duffy. And of course, any literary history of imagined authorship must pay homage to the monumental and brilliant work of the Portuguese poet Fernando Pessoa (1888-1935), whose forty-four heteronyms—invented characters over whose signature the poems appeared—account for almost three-fourths of his life's work.

More complicated, the publication of poetry under a false name or a nom de plume—such as W.D. Snodgrass' anagrammatic use of S.S. Gardons, "author" of the charmingly entitled 1970 volume *Remains,* published by the equally charmingly named Perishable Press—invites us to pay no attention to the man behind the screen, at least until such time as the text's provenance becomes known. Yet another possibility exists for fabricating a self, a more subversive and perverse approach, and that is the hoax, of the kind most notably perpetrated by the bored Australian soldiers Lieutenant James McAuley and Corporal Harold Stewart in 1943, whose invented poet, Ern Malley, had his Modernist poems championed by an equally invented sister, Ethel. More recently, another hoax has renewed our faith in skepticism—the forging, oft-attributed to the American Kent Johnson, of a non-existent Hiroshima survivor and poet, Araki Yasusada.

But *The Imaginary Poets* offers another way to think about the writer as ventriloquist, one both serious and carnivalesque: the contributors here have written poems that needed to be "translated" first, that is, written as though translated from another language. As a result, the ways in which these poets see their imagined others offer a distorted view that also constitutes a self-portrait of sorts. What is "translated" as an act of imagining might thus be understood as the self seen prismatically through an act of imagined translation.

Readers familiar with the poems of any of these writers will surely find affinities between their self-signed work and the work of their imagined poets; perhaps it is perverse and true that no matter what we do, we cannot run from ourselves, even though we can hide. Such affinities between the "original" poetry and the works here were, in part, the impetus for this project: from the outset, *The Imaginary Poets* has aimed to inform the reading of its contributors' self-signed works, to tell us more about the poets whose imaginations have been excited by this call to charms.

Other affinities abound. A number of contributors have chosen World War II as the scrim for their projections, and depicted in moving fashion various crimes perpetrated during the Holocaust, a few of the poems written from the point of view of victims and others from that of the oppressor. Something might well be made of these decisions, were a reader to be inclined to psychological analysis. The writing of political poetry, at times self-censored as a result of a given poet's own lack of suffering, here finds an outlet, the imagination allowing for a shift in content (if not subject). What one can imagine, after all, turns out to be horrific.

Not incidentally, many of the imaginary poets collected here are dead. Perhaps a reader might see this phenomenon as mere coincidence in light of the volume's limited sample, and how the affinities among the entries could be treated as anecdotal rather than empirical evidence. But one might also understand the coincidence as emblematic: the past remains many poets' great subject after all, the present turned into the past as soon as writing happens, the future unknowable. To imagine a dead speaker is to allow oneself access to the past without the problem of nostalgia—to avoid idealizing experience simply because it was one's own, trauma and triumph aggrandized alike.

But the rendering of an experience in these scratches and scritches called "words" necessarily fails to be the experience itself, a notion Plato knew too well, the poets barred from the Republic on the grounds of their dissembling. Words might be a problem, as such. And so, another affinity between the various entries in this volume bears noting, and that is, the number of poems presented as a version of something lost, in the tradition of the signifier as palimpsest. When asked to invent, the poets here responded cheerily, and their inventions were full of delightful moments of absence, slippage, and decentering. Poetry does happen in such moments as well, and yet the preponderance of those moments within the construction of these imaginary cultural artifacts speaks directly to the ways in which language isn't "real," a notion the authors of *The Imaginary Poets* understand.

And thus, with serious glee, here they are: the poets the poets have imagined. I wish them and you, dear reader, well.

Alan Michael Parker

The
IMAGINARY POETS

Aliki Barnstone as

Eva Victoria Perera 1

The Blue House

I can see a long way up here
where the blue house is balanced
on a bluff yellow with late summer
fields that extend to the city.

You can see me, for the door
and the windows are open to air.

I sit in a chair and hold a cup
of tea. Or is that you I see inside
and is that me, running downhill,
away from the house, on the path

lined with hip-high wheat.
Looming larger above me

the closer I come is the jumble
of buildings, a white cross atop
each sky-blue dome, the church
enclosed by Byzantine battlements.

Is that figure below the cathedral,
almost too small to see,

raising an arm toward the city
in joy? Or turning back
to wave goodbye to the house?
Why does the modest cottage

seem so isolated from town?
Why is it painted such a radiant blue?

The wood looks like the glass
of the evil eye, and the planes
aren't square, but ramshackle.
The foundation is shored up

against the hill, on the brink—
I can see the danger now.

And yet the blue house
invites us to look in, enter,
have a seat and drink
a cup of tea that tastes

too beautiful on the tongue
when you exclaim, "Ah, the view!"

The house was not blue.
My memory painted it
the color of the morning sea.
Look, out there, far from shore,

the fisherman is
disappearing in his orange boat

that floats along a gray smear
of light, marring the sapphire depths.
In the impossible pigment
is the day we have to leave

for good, to find other refuge.
No, the blue house was not

a hue in nature, sea or sky
or a precious stone.
It was a color made
by human hands, like a home.

Eva Victoria Perera (1917–2001)

EVA VICTORIA PERERA was the daughter of a well-to-do jeweler and importer, Jacobo, and a pianist, Sophia. Jacobo Angel was a descendent of the Sephardic Jews who came to Thessaloniki after 1492. He met Sophia in Vienna where she was studying piano. Jacobo traveled widely and was passionate about the arts and intellectual inquiry. An unconventional man, he rejected subservient roles for women and was attracted to Sophia's strong will, humor, and musical talent. In 1937, Eva married Isaak Perera, a talented piano student of her mother's. In 1939, their daughter, Eleftheria, was born. The young couple lived with Eva's parents after their marriage. Isaak became an architect.

When the Germans invaded Greece in 1942, Jacobo had the wherewithal to buy the immediate family false Christian identities. They fled to the island of Andros, where they were taken in by Christian friends. After the war, nearly all their friends and relatives were dead; 50,000 Jews from the city known as "The Mother of Israel" perished in Auschwitz. The Pereras found the ghosts too painful and left Thessaloniki to settle in Athens. Eventually, they bought land on Andros, and built a home there. Eva wrote poetry all her life, though like Cavafy she never printed her work for the public, only for her friends. After Eleftheria grew up, Eva withdrew to the island. She spent her last years devoted to "growing an Eden" in her garden, where she loved to have outdoor dinner parties for her family and friends.

Writing Poetry with Eva Victoria Perera

The summer of 2002, I was at a dinner party on the island of Serifos, talking to a mother and daughter whom I had just met. Our conversation turned to poetry, and I told them I was working on a translation of C.P. Cavafy. Elefthería, the mother, was excited to hear about my project, and told me that she and her daughter, Sophia, were editing a volume of her mother's collected poems, to be published for the first time next year. "If you love Kavafis so much, and are so deeply influenced by him," Sophia chimed in, "perhaps you would be interested in translating the poems of my grandmother, Eva Victoria Perera. There's a strange kinship between them." With some reluctance—I hadn't heard of her—I gave them my address in the States so that they could send the book to me when it was published. Maybe I had drunk too much, or maybe it was that Eva had died a year earlier, or that she was published by Ikaros, which also brought out the work of Seferis and Ritsos, or maybe it was curiosity. I'd never met any Greek Jews before, and Perera was a Sephardic Jew from Thessaloniki who survived the Holocaust.

I received a copy of *Eva's Voice* in early 2003, the dark time when America was going to war with Iraq. I was getting emails from my dear friends, who had shared that auspicious table with me, saying that anti-Americanism in Greece, indeed, in all Europe, "was out of bounds." Perhaps I should, one suggested, write a letter and send it to the Greek newspapers to show the perspective of a "good American." Though I knew my friends in Greece distinguished between me personally and my country's foreign policy, I was beside myself. The book arrived just when I needed most to hear poetry which deals with suffering and ordinary, domestic beauty. In Perera's work I heard the voice of a survivor who feels guilt, shame, empathy, joy to be alive, to be among the lucky, while others suffer and die. As Eva's biography and work reveal, she survived through a combination of privilege and good luck. (Although there were many well-off Jews in Thessaloniki, less than four percent survived.) Yet simply surviving made her and her family objects of shame. As Joshua Eli Plaut writes: "Nobody welcomed the survivors home.... People in Salonika referred to the Jews back from deportation as 'unused cakes of soap.'"

Though, of course, the circumstances are crucially different, I, too, am lucky to be alive, to be able to write poems, and live among loved ones, while others are afflicted in unspeakable ways. You, too, as readers of this essay, are similarly lucky. But the privilege of life, I surmise, is mere chance, and not a reward, not controllable, not the destiny of a nationality, not evidence of grace. Those justifications might save me from living in fear, but they also might prevent me from empathizing with others who through accident, do not share my good fortune. *Eva's Voice* showed me a way to explore this ethical and philosophical conundrum.

Sophia had hinted at the odd affinity between Cavafy and Perera. Both poets are "poet-historians" who recount the past from the individual's perspective. Cavafy's poetry is internal, whether he speaks for Antony or for a poor traveling salesman who in a rioting crowd hears "the gigantic lie / from the palace—Antony triumphed in Greece." Both combine an intensely personal voice with an analysis of the political. Perera wrote: "My aim is tell the stories of the past, whether ancient or twentieth century, so that they describe the now, as well. And I wish to record the voices of Greek people, Christian and Jewish, who lived through the second world war." Both poets came from cities, Alexandria and Thessaloniki, where Muslim, Christian, and Jewish cultures came together and flourished. Cavafy was a homosexual, Perera a Jew, so each was seen to be an outsider. Both poets frequently delineate the anatomy of alienation and connection, and how connection can degenerate into hostility, once group doctrine defines it. In their works, we feel the dehumanizing effect of sectarian identity when it erases individual identity, as when Perera writes: "I think, they know who I am, and they'll take me away. / At last, they've identified me, however narrowly."

The two poets also share an erotic poetics, embodied in the following lines from Cavafy's poem, "Outside the House":

> suddenly the charm of love made everything beautiful,
> the shops, the sidewalks, stones,
> and walls and balconies and windows;
> nothing ugly remained there.

Perera writes of these lines: "Isn't this spiritual and bodily love, which animates everything and universally imparts its beauty the ultimate affirmation of life?" Yet in the way they portray the physical and sensory world, Cavafy and Perera are crucially different. Cavafy describes the bodies of lovers, but he tends to focus on the exquisite details of the interactions between people. There are almost no landscapes or cityscapes in his work. Perera's erotic poetics include color, panorama, surreal visual juxtapositions, and a desire to create with words the plasticity of the external world.

This distinction between the two poets arises, perhaps, from Perera's lifelong love of the visual arts, and her work as an amateur painter. She was particularly drawn to another Holocaust survivor, Marc Chagall, whom she first met in 1952, when he visited Greece. Perera records that in their conversations Chagall said, "I was accused of falling into literature.... What I call 'abstract' is something that rises spontaneously from a gamut of psychic and plastic contrasts, bringing to the picture and to the eye of the spectator realizations of the unknown objects." She replied that her poems arose from "a descent into wordlessness, into the sensory and visual, which can be as fearful and painful as it is joyful.... I regard naming the physical world as preservation and as memory. How else can we be redeemed?" In one of Perera's many homages to Chagall, "Red Picnic, 1946," she writes:

> There are no houses turned upside down.
> There's the carafe of burgundy on the red blanket
> And just a little food. A tomato. An end of bread.
>
> So much beauty, to name it feels almost like peace,
> like sorrow to name it, too, as if my words
> could save the picture of you smiling at us...

In these lines, and in other poems, she depicts ordinary, domestic life as beautiful and strange. There is an ominous quality in the negative, "There are no houses turned upside down." As in "Day Breaks on Andros, 1944," "Picnic" implicitly asks the questions, "Why them and not me? Why do I get to have a picnic after the war, when others were taken away, their homes pillaged?" In "Andros" the speaker takes me inside just such a fear of abduction; she is "almost afraid to reassure herself" that her daughter is sleeping peacefully in the bed beside her. There's also an implied shame in that the speaker and her family pose as Christians, in order to be "passed over."

Eva's Voice turns me to face the possibility of a divine void. If I think of others suffering, then think, "There but for the grace of God..." I entertain the notion that I'm chosen for a destiny. I see that the simplest things in my daily life I enjoy by chance: taking my daughter to the park, driving a car, having water for lawns, switchings on the electric lights when I prepare supper at night.

Days of 2003

Here's a minute of my jubilation before the blue dwindles
and falls to the flowers of the desert willow
and falls onto the boulders on the mountain summit.
She'd been riding her bike in the park, tracing a helix
on the sidewalk that runs through the grass, a fiction
of a lawn, really, a little heaven made by sprinklers.
Her index finger is hooked in the collar of her princess t-shirt.
She smiles at me, off-guard, just for an instant
before losing patience and running from the camera,
climbing on a swing, stretching her strong legs to the sky,
before we get in the car to go home for dinner,
before I think, "count your blessings," and am ashamed.
As if we were chosen. Here's a picture of my daughter
just before the sun sinks, igniting fires along the borders
of a purple cloud. Here's a day, and our ordinary luck.

Josh Bell as *Saurah Joan Mao* [9]

New Year's Letter from a Guerilla Encampment in Chiapas (On the Eve of Revolution)

Greetings, 1994: please add the Mao
household to the list of coming
jihads. Eve did her time in the garden,
soon went skipping through
the barn. Guilty me, I burn
the bed I lie in, a fever of vampires
in the looking glass, my lines
turning on each other, like dogs,
in the poems I've left behind. Eduardo

and Elena, transitive/intransitive
inside the watchtower, the watchtower
stuck up black and like a rationale
against the puppet forehead
of the sky. This year, infinity
shrank suspect in the grosbeak's
allegiances to sun: we marked
the supposed waltzes of the planets
and the robot's martial love song,

sung a night's long grandeur
to the canned heart of Mexico,
to the long summer bees now dead
and picking their furry coats
from trace constellations
of early snow. If you please,
Time, send your gift again
and again, another year of music
and archiloquy for me, of mermaid

skin and loss, a new knit cap
for Marcos, a better gun for all
our children, more sweet minutes
in the watchtower, our Dorics gone
to Pyrrhics in an eyeblink. Don't
just stand there, brave there
like a specter hallooing in the tall
grass. Bring more war songs
spanking through the highlands.

Nuns on mescaline. Eduardo
the prankster. Mules in a tizzy, my
Marcos vague and handsome
in last year's knit cap, stalwart,
(I haven't had the time to knit
another one) his pretty eyes
unleashing their sidelong
ballotade across me, saying *maybe*
poetry is the ghost you fucked
who didn't want to fuck you (such

language) or *maybe you limp*
in time with the grosbeak, your body
fails you into flight. But even mock
poetic, Marcos knows my broken knee
knows better, calls winter Winter,
grinds down shameless and Aeolian
as I walk the encampment
toward the cliff, the cartilage gristed
like wheat between the bones

and oh, that I could break my body
open, and feed us on that song.
For now, prayers, broad portents:
stiff and cryogenic frogs lurking
in the wells, Coyolxauhqui[1] weeping
from the mountain's stone face,
weird her loving transom, spilled
catchall down the valleyways,
and tomorrow we descend
into the villages with guns. And whose
body catching yours, child, in

the continental drift? The singular god
who used to sign his autograph
on any bit of sky we'd hand him
has left a hole in the stage. So whose
heart discovered, through the chest,

---

[1]Coyolxauhqui (C): Aztec goddess of the moon. C was dismembered by her brother, Huitzilopochtli (H), for killing their mother. H threw C's head into the sky (which became the moon) and tossed her dismembered body down the mountain. Typical of Mao to borrow widely from any tradition at hand: note her use of the pain in her knee as "Aeolian," and the reference to Islamic jihad.

in the oldest of ways, voluminous
and strange? For my apology,
please walk the 100 westward paces
from the city's indecipherable
skeleton, to the blank green phrase
of jungle, where you'll pick out

my charitable failures from
the pocket of the earth. For my
apology, please forward fifty river girls
to Marcos, the soft girls washing
their clothes on stones, their legs
folded clean as stone below them
and clean as stone their voices
lift in song, skin dark and penetrable
as their own quick logic, of which logic
I have never burned inside. These girls
they will be brave, they will remain
beautiful and convinced, will have

the hands and nerves enough
to keep him dreadful and aligned.
I could not. I could barely keep
my trousers from tearing
on the barbed wire, and if you were
to drop me from an airplane
I am the kind of girl to turn back,
weightless, toward you, to study
your face as it grew smaller, forgetting
the push and your betrayal, forgetting

the earth as it leapt up bigger,
like a fish, bald and blue
through the tensile surfaces
of nearer space. In other news,
I am not sorry for attempting
to throw the world away: where
the metal kissed the metal, and in
the clockwork guts of it, it always
seemed disposable, built to be abandoned,
proud with our name on its lips
and spoke us into wind and girls,

and praised us for our enfilades
and ducked inside us, kept us for
the morning song. True, I am a tourist
here. In his passion, Marcos
calls me white-girl, my blond hair
a magnet for the snipers. But it is true
that I could kill everything I see:
the girl in love with the boy,
the boy who has a sister, the sister
splashing in the mountain lake,

sure and alive in the interchangeable
sleeve of skin she's saving up
for the next neoteric soul. Draw your bow
across her body, drop your sights
upon her, watch her lessen
in the black plunder of the earth,

a lot of water underneath the bridge,

a lot of poison in the meat,

and braver still the heart I've borrowed,

from time to time, to love you

through the trigger, when the lines

in the poem I wasn't writing

came clicking like insects for me

across the tile, casting their gravid

alphabet at my feet, some seeds

planted upside down, green priests

lost toward Australia. I always

thought we'd die picking locks

with the stems of pretty flowers,

with the names of pretty flowers

still sticking from our mouths,

gutting fish before we turn them loose,

watching them spiral into bloodless

mountain lakes. And now Elena

filling up the feed bags, Marcos

handsome in the knit cap, the mules

gone crazy with mercury, the lava thoughtful

because it holds. Let me add my name

to the list of the conscious: life

comes up green and ugly

from the jungle floor, forces us

to breathe it, and whosoever
reads this letter, put your spoon
down easy. Less than music
comes the morning, the mules
dying and the bread gone, the thousand
count of all our changeless eyes
closing mindlessly as scissors
on the Capitol, the better part
of our beautiful alphabet
sweet and echoless in grass.

SAURAH JOAN MAO (1969–1995)

CHIAPAN REVOLUTIONARY Saurah Joan Mao (born Adelita Blanco) lived a fantastic life which continues to overshadow her work as a poet. Born in Las Margaritas, Mexico, in 1969, to a Belgian nun who died during childbirth and an American stuntman later convicted of murder in Ciudad Juarez, she was raised by the Margaritas Highland nuns, from whom she broke at the age of fourteen. At fifteen, she attempted suicide by jumping from the top of a moving bus and into oncoming traffic, and at seventeen, now with her characteristic limp, she joined with the indigenous Zapatista Liberation Army of Chiapas (EZLN).

Though mistrusted by members of the EZLN because of her Anglo heritage (evidenced by her pale skin and yellow hair), young Adelita was fiercely critical of her government's treatment of its indigenous peoples, and in the EZLN encampments she began writing her first poems, apocalyptic manifestos against oppression. Their visionary authority helped win her acceptance as soldier and equal, and eight years later she married subcommandante Marcos Acuna, changed her name to Saurah Joan Mao, and published her single book of poems, *Untitled Resurrection Project.* In 1994 she took part in the EZLN's New Year's Revolution. In 1995, in a skirmish outside San Cristobal de las Casas, Mao was killed by federal soldiers, who believed they'd accidentally shot an anglo journalist. In her pocket was an unfinished letter to a woman named Juliet Montana, and a handwritten translation of Mayakovsky's "The Backbone Flute." She was twenty-six years old.

Saurah Joan Mao: Against The Robot's Martial Love Song

We think of the spirit as that which travels on without the body, past supposition. But unknown to the body, which moves always forward, my spirit stays behind with you, as if to keep my place.

From an unfinished letter to Juliet Montana, 1995

The Mexican poet who called herself Saurah Joan Mao[2] claimed—perhaps for political reasons—that her favorite poet was countryman Octavio Paz, and her work does bear signs of his impact; but in her journals and her letters to husband Marcos Acuna and lover Juliet Montana, no writer gets as much attention as English poet William Shakespeare. Mao studied his characters religiously, finding, in two of them, what she called "early prototypes" of the Mao personality: Cleopatra she described as the "first propagandist of the self"; and Macbeth— "the man for whom the thing imagined was the thing beheld"—she loved for his flawed ambition, and for the proleptic fervor of his imagination. Both the poet and the revolutionary, she seemed to be saying to us, must envision the self as a powerful imaginative commodity, and this imaginative commodity must be able, itself, to imagine the unforeseeable future—the new regime, the coming poem— as having occurred the very moment it was imagined.

Therefore, since she brandished herself as such a commodity, a propagandist of self, anything you've heard about her is likely untrue, for what biography we know of Saurah Joan Mao, we know from her own contradictory letters, and from her strange, compulsive memoirs, of which she wrote three, none of them completed and all of them seemingly written by, and about, vastly different women. Here's an example, a story of her early life, from her first memoir, *The Incomplete Mao* (though written by Mao, it's delivered in third person):

> In a field behind the nunnery of the Margaritas Highlands,
> Saurah Joan Mao (then the orphan prodigy Adelita Blanco) had
> her first vision of the Virgin Mary, who appeared dressed in full
> armor and carrying a shining sword with which she beheaded
> scarecrows, and which shining sword then blinded little Adelita,
> as if it were the sun itself.

---

[2]"Mao" is the Chinese revolutionary; "Joan" is the virgin prophet; and "Saurah" is an Arabic name meaning of, or like, the sun.

Later, in one of her letters to Juliet Montana, Mao would claim she'd been literally blinded by this vision, and never regained her sight until the onset of menstruation. Furthermore, in this same letter (though she doesn't mention it in any of the memoirs), Mao claims the Virgin, as if in apology for striking her blind, accompanied her until she regained her sight, as a kind of ephemeral seeing-eye dog, going so far as to read "from the Bible aloud to [her] at night."

But it only gets stranger: though born in Mexico, though fiercely patriotic, she was the child of a Belgian nun (who died during childbirth) and an American stuntman (who later died in prison). She was raised by the nuns of Las Margaritas, who educated her in three languages and reportedly beat her into *petit mal* seizures. She was a runaway, an illegitimate white pariah. She attempted suicide twice. She began writing manifestos at the age of twelve. She endlessly predicted her own death. She was a revolutionary with the Zapatista Liberation Army of Chiapas (EZLN) by age sixteen. Because of her Anglo heritage, her revolutionary fellows mistrusted her—as did most of her countrymen—up to the day she gave her life for them. She was probably bipolar, definitely bisexual, and loved the mysterious— and, some scholars say, entirely fictional—Juliet Montana, the only consistent feature of all three memoirs. But she married subcommandante Marcos Acuna, who wrote this famous sentence about her in his journal: "Adelita [he called her nothing else] has no top to her head: the very second an idea enters it, it connects immediately with the sky." Shortly after this was written, she took part in the EZLN New Year's revolution. That year she published her single book, *Untitled Resurrection Project,* written in a surreal, apocalyptic, yet highly personal voice, which she later termed, in a letter to Acuna, the Inanimate Subjective. Mao believed the poet/revolutionary should speak and write as if she were already dead; therefore her voice was the voice, she claimed, "of an inanimate subjective, a dead thing—a rock, a tree, an angel—unnecessarily articulate." A year later, she was killed by federal troops outside San Cristobal de las Casas. There are only two adult photos of her, one taken postmortem by the soldiers who killed her—her body so small, the metal table she lies upon could fit two more of her across—and one, taken in an EZLN encampment, which shows her laughing, sunburnt, and carrying an ancient carbine.

Finally, though, the poems are the unassailable truth of Saurah Joan Mao. I found them by sheer luck: in 1999, at a book fair in Mexico City, a friend of mine, the

Canadian poet Matthew Guenette, stumbled across a copy of Mao's book, *Untitled Resurrection Project,* and knowing that to me it was the holy grail—one heard of it everywhere, read it nowhere—he sent it to me. Here are the first lines I read and translated, a self-written inscription for her tombstone:

> In case of Revelation, do not resurrect,
> for I have teased, until weeping, the war-bird Jehova,
> for they have killed me in Mexico, where they translate my bones
> into diamonds, and then make love to the tenured white frog of Justice.

One hears, here, the self-critical ravings of Lear, the breadth of Whitman through Cardenal, and a lucid, violent surreality which belongs to no one else. A "political" poet, her political poems never seem political, as in "The Song of *The Song of Songs,"* her poem, of revolution and eroticism, written for Marcos Acuna:

> It's true that we are yet evolving
> into still more degradable
> wonders, one body
> more musical than living, the next
> more acceptable
> than ash.

Here she speaks of the body's sacrifice—to the lover, to the revolution—and she's able to keep her mind on the benefit of that sacrifice—that eventual evolution of ash—while never delving into death worship or deluded romanticism. In this poem, and the poem "New Year's Letter" (translated above), I find Mao at her most vibrant and various. These poems, like the person, rage, dazzle, reject, digress, return, attack. But it is "New Year's Letter," finally, which is her flagship song of love and pain, created to defy what she calls "the robot's martial love song," that failure of imagination which her fellow visionary William Blake embodied in the figure of Urizen, and more than any other contemporary poet I know, Mao created a poetic voice—"a rock, a tree, an angel"—which is up to the demands of the future and the past.

Mi-Novembre

Le dernier de nos hommes est parti aujourd'hui:
Pierre-le-borgne, le vieil aiguiseur de couteaux,
la baïonnette au dos, en route pour le maquis
au delà des vignes, dans les grottes des côteaux.

Nous voilà donc seules à Sainte-Marie-des-Ifs,
sans amants, sans maris. Les Allemands avancent
vers le Midi. J'ai peur qu'ils trouveront les Juifs
cachés depuis deux ans chez la vieille Constance:

leur pauvre nouveau-né de cesse de pleurer,
né dans cette cave sans lumière; si seulement
nous pouvions être sûres que la fille des Bonnier
ne nous dénonçe pas je prendrais leur enfant

chez nous: Marie est trop petite pour parler.
Hier, à la craie sur le tableau noir, j'ai transcrit
un poème de Goethe, un autre de Mallarmé:
peut-être y aura-t-il quelques soldats parmi

eux qui y verront un geste et se souviendront
que ce qui nous sépare n'est qu'une langue, après tout.

Dehors, les enfants jouent à la récréation,
chantent et rient au soleil qui semble ignorer tout

de la guerre, et voudrait nous parler du présent,
nous dire d'ignorer l'approche de l'ennemi—
et si Dieu faisait qu'il ne passent pas par ici?
Comme ce matin est beau, et comme l'espoir me prend.

16 November, 1943

Mid-November

The last of our men left today:
one-eyed Peter, old sharpener of knives,
bayonet on his back, en route for the Maquis
beyond the vineyard, in the hill's caves.

We are alone now, in Sainte Marie des Ifs,
without lovers or husbands. The Germans advance
southwards. I fear the Jews will come to grief,
hidden these two years in the home of old Constance.

Their poor newborn infant cries incessantly.
I would take their child, born in that lightless
cellar, home to my place—if only
the Bonnier's daughter wouldn't betray us—

because Marie is still too small to talk.
Yesterday, on the school's blackboard, I copied out
a poem by Goethe, and one by Mallarmé in chalk—
maybe a few soldiers among that rout

will see a gesture in this and quickly guess
that only language separates us. Nothing more.
Outside, the children play at recess,
laugh and gambol in the sun that seems to ignore

the menace, and speaks only of our present scope,
urging us to forget the approaching enemy—
and what if God contrived to steer them all away?
How beautiful the morning, now I'm seized with hope.

Mid-November *(Alternate Translation)*

Mid-November. The last of our men left today:
one-eyed Peter, the old knife sharpener,
bayonnette on his back, en route for the maquis
beyond the vineyards, in the hill's caves.

We are alone now, in Sainte-Marie-des-Ifs
without lovers or husbands. The Germans
advance toward the South. I fear for the Jews
hidden for two years at old Constance's:

their newborn never ceases to cry,
born in that lightless cellar. If only
we could be certain the Bonnier's daughter
wouldn't denounce us, I would take their child

with me: Marie is still too small to talk.
Yesterday, in chalk on the blackboard, I transcribed
a Goethe poem, and another by Mallarmé—
maybe a few soldiers among them

will see a gesture in this and remember
that what separates us is only language, after all.
Outside, at recess, the children play,
play and laugh in the sun that seems to ignore

the war and wants to speak only of the present,
telling us to ignore the approaching enemy—
and what if God contrived they didn't come this way?
How beautiful this morning, how hope seizes me.

ANNE-MAËLLE MATHIEU (1911–1943)

ANNE-MAËLLE MATHIEU was born, lived and died in Sainte-Marie-des-Ifs, a tiny vineyard village North of the Lubéron region in France. She was the Mayor's daughter and from 1939 until her death the only school teacher in the village's one-room schoolhouse. She was the author of a poetry collection *Chantemerle* and of a book of short stories, *Trois Chiens (Three Dogs),* which won the Prix Airique in 1939.

From 1939 to 1943—during the years of WWII—she wrote *Les Gestes de la Mémoire (The Gestures of Memory).* The seventy poems in this book, all in alexandrines, narrate the life of the village and the activities of the region's *Résistance* movement, of which she was an active member, relaying messages between the three local factions, and printing, on the school's roneo machine, tracts that were distributed throughout the Lubéron. Her husband, Guillaume Mathieu, the village doctor and vintner, was the founder and leader of *Groupe 77*, the most active regional *Résistance* group, responsible mainly for the dispersion of underground news and radio transmissions. He was drafted by the French Army in 1942 to work at the Military Hospital of LeBrun, thirty kilometers away from Sainte-Marie-des-Ifs.

Anne-Maëlle Mathieu was shot by the Germans in the village square on November 17, 1943. Published posthumously, *Les Gestes de la Mémoire* won the prestigious Prix Burchelle in 1945.

On Anne-Maëlle Mathieu

On November 17, 1943, six months before the end of WWII, the Germans invaded the tiny French village of Sainte-Marie-des Ifs. They soon discovered that—with the exception of two old and disabled men—only women and a small number very young children lived there. The Germans assembled everyone in the town square and started interrogating the women to find out where the village's men were hiding. Most of the women replied that they were unmarried, widowed, or that their husbands had enlisted in or been drafted by the French Army. But later that night, one of the women—in exchange for her and her son's immunity—told the Germans that Constance Dechutère, Anne-Maëlle Mathieu's neighbor and *Résistance*-friend, was hiding a Jewish family in her cellar. The German's modus operandi then was to execute three villagers for each Jew they found. The Jewish couple and their infant, as well as six women and three children, were shot in the village square that night. Among the executed were Anne-Maëlle Mathieu, her two-year-old daughter Marie, and their neighbor Constance Dechutère. It was later discovered that Anne-Maëlle's sister had fled that very morning with twenty-one of the village's older children and had made it to the hills where the local *Résistance* was hiding.

Five months later, in April 1945, just before the end of WWII, poet & novelist Louis Aragon and Jean Cassou, a novelist and critic, met in the offices of the *Revue Europe-Liberté* in Paris, to discuss the project of editing an anthology of French *Résistance* poetry. Aragon had just returned from Lyon where he had met with the leaders of Southern France's resistance. Among them was Guillaume Mathieu, Anne-Maëlle Mathieu's husband, and the head of the *Résistance* unit *Groupe 77*. He told Aragon about his wife and the other women and children's fate, and gave Aragon a copy of A.-M. Mathieu's roneo-typed manuscript *Les Gestes de la Mémoire (The Gestures of Memory)*. Aragon took the manuscript to Paris and showed it to David Rohan, also a French *Résistance* and the Managing Editor of *Les Editions Unies,* who published it in March of 1946. That same year it won the famous Prix Burchelle, and was later translated into Dutch, Italian, and Spanish. Only a few poems were translated in English and published in the United States, namely in *Literary Page* (in 1950), *Three Roads* (1950), and *Stanza Quarterly* (1952). To my knowledge "Mid-November" was never translated.

***

A few words on my work in translating this poem. At first, I wrote a free, more literal translation of "Mid-November,"—which preserved the stanza form but not the rhyme scheme or syllabic count of the alexandrine. But the result didn't have the formal, heightened tone of A-M. Mathieu's poem. I then tried, as often as possible, to restore the classical meter of the French, twelve-syllable alexandrine line, and attempted to restore the rhyme scheme without violating the general sense of the poem. This required the re-arrangement of certain lines and stanzas. For example, in the first line, I needed four more syllables to have an alexandrine, so I took the liberty of repeating the title as the two first words of the line.

In stanza three I moved information around quite a bit, but the overall meaning expressed remains the same. I also played it fast and loose with the rhyme scheme in this stanza, off-rhyming "lightless" with "betray us."

In the second line of stanza four, instead of simply saying "transcribed" to literally translate *"transcrit,"* I preferred "copied out," but then the rhyme in line four required I insert something not in the original French: "that rout." But, again, the spirit of the original is preserved. This kind of invention recurs in the last stanza, where I changed "this moment" to "our present scope," a phrase obviously not in the original French poem, which has only *"du présent,"* "of the present." But I knew I wanted the poem to end on the word "hope," instead of trailing off with "seizes me," even though this is faithful to the original French, *"me prend."*

Of course, the English version also naturally falls into an iambic gait—in the penultimate line for example—but that's all to the better, I think, for the formal feel of the poem. In the original poem, each line is an alexandrine. In my translated version, there are only ten. But of the remaining lines, there are five "almost alexandrines" (eleven syllables), and two hyper-metric lines, as thirteen syllables. So the overall metrical feel of the poem in English is more alexandrine than not. There are ten-syllable lines mixed in, one of them a perfect pentameter: " because Marie is still too young to talk," which reflects the classical English metric.

The final line is not only an alexandrine, but has a caesura after the seventh syllable, almost exactly where it would appear in the classic French system. By preserving the rhyme scheme and trying to preserve more of the metrical system, I hope that *Mid-November* will reflect the formal, emotionally charged atmosphere of the original better than a looser, prosier translation.

Waters

Bridges cross with caution
Rivers resist the sea

Sea rattles the shore
Far from the rearing mountains

Sky rains bombs on fields
Rain makes ponds from craters

Someday fish will fill the ponds
The waters will be ours

HỘI AN (fl. mid-20ᵗʰ c.)

HỘI AN is the pseudonym of a poet who is identified in a 1972 biographical statement as a woman living in Viet Nam. Although some of the love poems seem to support the gender claim, serious doubts about her identity remain.

Hội An's work was published in France in the early seventies; because the poems appeared bilingually (with French translations), some readers have suggested that they were actually written by a French critic of the American War who had his or her own poems "translated" into Vietnamese. The relative quality of the poems and translations argues against this, and the poems themselves suggest that Hội An was deeply familiar with Vietnamese culture and landscape.

But if Hội An was living in Viet Nam, why wasn't her work published there? Though somewhat more oblique, poems like "Waters" are consistent in attitude with other poems being written in Viet Nam at the time. And Hội An's pseudonym has Vietnamese counterparts, including that of the poet Thu Bồn (1935-2003), who named himself for the river that flows through the small town for which Hội An named herself.

The town itself suggests a third possibility. One of the oldest cities in Southeast Asia, Hội An was a major international port where Asian and European traders came until late in the nineteenth century; it was also an administrative center for French colonials. Perhaps, as others have speculated, Hội An was an overseas Vietnamese *(Việt-kiều)* who had gone to France before the American War; perhaps she found in the ancient town a connection between what had become her two cultures, as well as a symbol of the longing she felt for her native country.

On "Waters" by Hội An

Partly out of a desire to understand the devastation of a distant country more deeply than the news allowed, I wrote some of my first poetry during the Viet Nam War. One now-lost poem tried to "invent" a Vietnamese woman, but became in essence a series of questions (does she walk through a field? does she carry a gun?) that were answered with the refrain "I do not know."

Since then I've come to know a number of Vietnamese women, as well as a number of poets whose work gives me some sense of what it was and is like to live in Viet Nam. But the process of actually translating Vietnamese poems has taken me beyond even this kind of "news," challenging me with what I've come to call the problem of "translating emotion" and at the same time giving me, by immersion in a language so different from my own, a sense of linguistic and poetic possibilities that English cannot easily claim.

Wherever Hội An's "Waters" was written, its author has clearly experienced the culture and geography of Viet Nam. The town of Hội An, for many years a port connected to the sea by the Thu Bồn River that flows through it, is an especially watery place. There are a number of bridges, including the famous Japanese covered bridge that connects the Japanese and Chinese quarters of the town. The second line of the poem, "Rivers resist the sea," may on one level reflect the difficulty experienced late in the nineteenth century, when the Thu Bồn became too shallow to navigate and Da Nang (familiar to Americans from the War) replaced Hội An as a major port. The "rearing mountains" of the fourth line also reflect the geography of Hội An, which is located on the south-central coast, with the famous Marble Mountains (including one known as "Heaven") visible in the north.

But the images of the poem evoke more than geography. "Bridges cross with caution" creates an almost surreal image by what appears to be a displacement of feeling, and the "resisting" rivers may suggest the response of the country itself to the influx of invaders from overseas. Both the "rattle" of the third line and the "rearing" of the fourth suggest uncustomary tension, a reading that is intensified by knowledge of the Vietnamese creation myth that tells of the coming together of the male sea and the female mountains (an interesting reversal of Western expectations). That rivers serve less as boundaries than as opportunities in Vietnamese agriculture, economy, and thought is also important for appreciating the poem.

The most significant reference to water, as well as the most challenging problem for the translator, is the title itself, which is repeated in the final line. In Vietnamese, the word for "country" and "water" is the same—*nước*. This is not a linguistic accident, but a reflection of the central role that all "waters" have played in the long history of the country. Following the third stanza, which reflects a phenomenon common in Viet Nam since the American bombing and which other poets have also described (see for example Lâm Thị Mỹ Dạ's "Bomb Crater Sky"), it is both possible and important to hear the last line of the poem as "The country will be ours"—a choice which the French translation makes (*il pays sera à nous*). But "country" ignores the water of the poem, which remarkably comes to include the ponds made by the American bombs; without something like "water" in the title and last line, the poem becomes more superficially political, less deeply and complexly felt. There are no articles in Vietnamese, but "the waters" seems to bring the final line close to the double meaning that is most apparent at the end of the poem, leaving the less specific "waters" to mark the beginning, where the ultimate focus is not yet apparent.

I have tried to make my translation suggest, though not imitate, the form of the original. Written in five-syllable lines, the poem is extremely condensed, reflecting both the form itself and the fact that the basically monosyllabic Vietnamese language has much less "connective tissue" than European languages. While inevitably increasing the number of syllables, I have used a mostly three-stress line to maintain the sense of form, and I have tried to keep the translation as spare as possible. (The French versions of "Waters" and other poems by Hội An, rendered in free verse, are more expansive, which is another reason for doubting that the poem was translated from the French.) Although the poem is written in the quatrains that are characteristic of many formal Vietnamese poems, the lines fall rather naturally into couplets, which I have chosen to use for the translation.

I hope that the challenge of condensing the English into a form that at least comes close to the original is met to some extent in the translation. It is true that the complexity of allusion and history experienced in virtually every line of the poem, and most especially in the word *"nước,"* can ultimately be experienced only by a native speaker—and, to a small extent, by the translator who has grappled with the poem. But there, in the single word of the title, is a reflection of both the rewards and limitations of all literary translation.

La Sagesse

Sa- wo

Wo-big

Wo-spu-ka-ka

Sa-wing-si-si

Peut-aller-comment

Montagne, cheval, J'entre maintenant

Wa-mu-fis-no

Clair tout fort

Go so wu nee

Wig wig won

Oooooooooooooooombaladindel,

Wokowanawonda

Hooooooooooooooo

nuage

Chant chant la sagesse

Chant tout fort
Ma-ma-beg-ma-sting

Ma ma kill kill

Pig ma ma

Sting roll will will scrapping foe

Foe foe foe bing bing la la

La le passereau

Vole vole suivez libre

Restant moi restant restant
Restant

Oooooooooooooooo!

Wisdom

Ba-ooo

oo-son

Oo-na-spi-spi

Bo-sa -nay-nay

May-go-how

Mountain, horse, I enter now

Ko-no-bin-day

Clear   Aloud

Fa on in kay

Sin sin so

Uuuuuuuuuuuuuurkinquinohaho

Basowindefun

Suuuuuuuuuuuuuuuuuuuuuu

Cloud

Sing sing wisdom

Sing aloud

Wo wo web wo wing

Wo wo ir ir

Ga wo wo

Nil cra boin boin palling giz

Giz giz giz mu mu sigh sigh

sigh swallow

Fly fly follow free

Remaining me remaining
remaining

Uuuuuuuuuuuuuuuuuu!

ROSE ELBOW SOURIS (1894–1969)

ROSE ELBOW SOURIS is the *nom de plume* of Nastasia Boulovogna, who was born in Kurdjali, Bulgaria in 1894. As a child, Souris began writing poems influenced by the Turkish ghazal singers; this experience with an unknown language may have been an early source of her fascination with pure poetic sound. The poet's family was scattered during the Second Balkan War, a period in Souris' life about which little is known except that it was when she adopted her new name. After the start of World War I she moved briefly to Zurich, where she met and influenced several Dada poets, most notably Hugo Ball. In 1919 she came to Paris, where she supported herself first as an artists' model and subsequently as a newspaper columnist and reporter.

Voix, Souris' first book of poetry, published in 1922, attracted notoriety in poetry circles. During the early 1920s, she also became known for frequent and mesmerizing spontaneous performances of her poems at cafés and salons. Like the poetry of Tristan Tzara and other Dada poets with whom she associated, Souris' poems appeared pure exercises in sound; but unlike them, she insisted that her work was fully meaningful in terms of a private code that she once described as "a voice to converse with the twin I lost at my birth."

In 1924, Souris' life and work changed forever when she became pregnant and had the first of three abortions. She spent the next decade completing the first two of her "Abortion Studies," poetic sequences that use the incantatory

power of sound to explore the personal and social reper-
cussions of her experience. Tragically, publishers of the time
found the *Etudes* too controversial to publish, and the
poems remained in manuscript for decades.

After a third abortion in 1935, Souris experienced a severe
psychotic break. The artist Nanette de Boursay brought her
friend to recover at her home in the country, where Souris
completed the third and final Abortion Study and pursued
her interest in the cultivation of plants, especially mush-
rooms. In October 1936 Souris vanished without warning. It
was commonly believed she had killed herself, but a dozen
years later, when her anonymously submitted book of
poems, *Wisdom,* won the Prix Nationale Poetry Award, it
was discovered that she had been living quietly as a truffle
farmer in the countryside near Limoges. She married a
young designer, Alain Restif, in 1944.

During the 1950s and '60s Souris maintained the truffle
farm, which she called Crux Solide and used also as the
home of a foundation for young women poets. During her
last decade, her contributions to poetry were recognized
with L'Aigle d'Or, Le Prix Louise Labé, Le Grand Prix de la
Société des Gens de Lettres, and other awards, and she won
election to the Academie Francaise. She died in 1969, leaving
behind several volumes of poems which were published
posthumously.

I first came across the name Rose Elbow Souris in Nanette du Boursay's famous "Portrait d'Une Fille," the girl whose face is obscured by the six cats is depicted with her elbow resting on a stack of books. The spine of the top book in the pile clearly bears the name "Souris," the only legible title among them, surmounted by a small embossed mouse. My search for that edition ended three years later at an antiquarian bookstore in Salamanca, Spain, where I also found other books of Souris' poetry. I was immediately taken by their charm and abandon, the unique blend of classical harmony and modernist rebellion. And as Souris' reputation has soared in recent decades, I have continued to learn from her poems and to revise and rethink my approach to translating her work.

In translating the poems, I concentrated on sound first, but tried to make myself a channel for the meanings as well. It took me months to translate my first four-line Souris lyric (the early fragment called, coincidentally, "Hymn to My Cat"). The challenge, as I saw it, was to avoid tipping too far towards the temptations of semantic violence, or forgoing Souris' delicate touch and direct respect for truth-telling. I am convinced that a subtext of allusion and connotation, woven into the words, would be easy to lose if too much emphasis were given to the play of sound.

Like Dickinson, Souris was obsessed with a difficult subject to which she kept returning; Souris' "flood subject," to use Dickinson's term for death, was, of course, abortion. Whether or not Souris' three abortions indicate a more-or-less-conscious need to face all the nuances of the experience—as one of her biographers has speculated—they did provide her with a sequence of new approaches to the theme. No other poet I know has found a way to treat the spiritual, psychological, and social ramifications of this subject with Souris' deft balance between awe and courage; her distinctive poetic voice, embodying freedom and reverence, seems a fitting vehicle. Much has been written recently on the sociology of abortion during Souris' lifetime—its illegality and the trauma surrounding it—and it is fitting that her poetry has been credited with helping change the climate for abortion, so that by 1988 the Health Minister of France could declare a new abortifacent "the moral property of women."

The earlier sections of Souris' abortion studies characteristically combine aleatory associativeness with lyric directness—as if two voices were talking together. By

contrast, many of the later sections are quite lucid and meditative, even philo-
sophical in scope, perhaps revealing the influence of Valéry, to whom Souris was
introduced soon after the publication of his *Charmes* in 1922 (there is no proof
for the speculation that Valery was the father of Souris' second aborted child, and
Souris was so private about her personal life that I doubt there ever will be). For
this book, I chose to translate one of the earlier sections of "Wisdom," the title
poem completed in the mid-1920s. I felt that the poem's distinctive blend of Dada
and lyric influences best captures the most essential flavor of Souris' work and her
initial fascination with her topic.

One of the most difficult decisions I faced was how to approach the translation
of certain sound-groups that have meanings in English: "beg," "kill," etc. I did
not want to censor any of the complexity of Souris' response to her material,
but in several cases, I felt the violent English connotations of the sounds would
interfere with the reader's apprehension of the core of the poem. It is well
established that Souris knew no English at all; indeed, her distaste for the
language and refusal to hear any of it became somewhat legendary. So, although
it is a coincidence of meaning that Valéry would have appreciated, I elected to
translate them into neutral sounds. Words that she clearly intended to have
meaning in French-*"montagne," "cheval," "nuage," "passereau"*—I have translat-
ed into their English equivalents.

Sweetest the Unexpected Sweet

And the stars
Stars the first night
Like virgin's soft unsuckled nipples chased
She gasped
Assuming only a man would find her doubt erotic

Her woman laughed
Lest she look back nostalgic
Nostalgic for catastrophe she laughed

And kneeling extravagantly for a woman to admire
Pearls
Unlikely variable reds ringed in her in
Myrrh
In milk and incense

Intermediaries
In the hesitations   yet no one told to stop
Falling toward unfamiliar try this slow tongue aflush

Another Moses moment stuttering

Stars

Stars the first night remind thy burning

Be

In this space of possibility she prayed

Transliteration:

And then there were many stars and she saw / that the stars the first night
though some were olives / others orange blossoms welcomed them eagerly
/ she clapped her hands / assuming the many tiny olive blossoms /
hung in air were guests to their fragrance and / privacy they laughed
for O the many / who find their pleasures / early on they danced
for O the men are absent / women dance they whispered crude and
unfamiliar / phrases shy in singing I like this try this /
without the instruments / between them of authority shy the /
healthy tongue initially and then the touch / the lily oil she spread and
secrecy / she bent her knees I / like the lotuses oil of crocuses / massaged with
such experience try this / the first night here and there unhurried the other
/ pleasures they will try

J II *(? - 561? B.C.E.)*

"J," OR "J I," TRADITIONALLY signifies the author of the older texts of the Pentateuch. That scribe lived some five hundred years before this second J and made indisputable contributions to literature. "J II" conveyed to earlier readers probably no more than an aesthetic lineage. The designations "J," "J I," or "the author of *The Book of J*," and "J II," or "Judith," or "the Auctrix," are, at best, inept; at worst, misleading. The word "Judith" translates "Jewess"; it is merely a generic gender indicator, a religious affiliation, not a clue that adequately inaugurates biography.

And just as J II has been taken for J I, she also has been called "Judith," after the character from her most well-known work, the Apocryphal *Book of Judith*. Until the discoveries of 1897, most readers attributed to J II the glories of her heroine: her incredible eloquence, intelligence, and the kind of charisma reserved for a god. They did not, for reasons lost to us, go on to attribute to J II her beautiful young heroine's military success: that she entered a wilderness, that she killed an enemy, that she defended her city and saved her people. Centuries after *Judith* was removed from the Bible, J II was still revered as the maker of this woman, this symbol of Israel.

Once her other poems, the "pagan" ones, were found in 1897 and then the second scroll in 1932, her "identity," beyond the simple fact of a woman writing, seemed less certain. Her most beloved poems are probably not the private yearnings of a solitaire but part of a ceremony for cultivated women. And whether she lived in the colony of Metapontum in Southern Italy or in Pompeii, as some have argued, or in Persia, most scholars agree that she died some distance from Jerusalem, independent of the Temple, and beyond the influence of her community.

Shifting Milieus; or, The Poem Translated

is considered, in passing, not unlike an olive-colored baby alligator lifted from its rock and shaken in the air by a bird, so that all the little bones break, and the baby is considered food now and eaten whole by the heron, which is also enchanting in its way, standing in the water, though the bird is not what the reader wants to remember.

*

Translators, in introducing their texts, sources, and the poet's excellence (and thus defending their considerable labor on behalf of the poet's immortality, or on behalf of culture, civility, or "international relations") usually begin with an apology and end with a hope. "I tried," the translator whimpers, which is fear, the common spur to apology. "I tried to find a way through two conflicting languages." And mea culpa, this is meant to absolve the apologist and, simultaneously, lower the language bar, low enough for hope, the oldest hope. To be heard. "I hope what follows introduces a new generation to the truth / the beauty / the strangeness of the poetry." In other words, admitting failure, I hope for mercy, since justice is not done to the original. Hope does not outweigh apology, unfortunately, and it is not what the reader wants to remember.

*

The poem, known generally as "Sweetest the Unexpected Sweet," is one way to introduce the next generation to J II's poetry. It is one of the poems discovered by archeologists in 1932. Since the last two lines were in Aramaic, and on a different bit of papyrus from the other Greek text, another twenty years would pass before any consensus developed on the integrity of the text. These "pagan" poems, as they were called, along with those unearthed near Pompeii in 1897, changed, significantly, the reception of her poetry, a change that might be useful to review.

Before 1897, J II was considered the author of the Apocryphal *Book of Judith* and a number of prayers too mutilated to evaluate. By 1921, most of the 1897 "pagan" poems were translated by English scientists, and those versions held contemporary attention about as long as did the poems of Margaret Mead. The sister of one of those scientists, though, one Edith Allison, amateur philologist, happened to be living with her brother, and it is to her that we owe our comparatively recent appreciation of J II's accomplishment. Allison saw the architecture among the poems, including *Judith,* the one long and the least mutilated poem. She saw that the Judith narrative contained some of the same elements as the Mysteries ancient women practiced in secrecy. I have written of this at length elsewhere and so have others (Gematria, 1933; Fierz-David, 1988; et al.). But it was Allison who first wrote persuasively on *Judith* as a bowdlerized document, one that traced a cultivated woman's initiation into the Dionysian, albeit coded and capable of passing into the Hebrew Bible. She argued for a definitive edition, with all the conventional scholarly apparatus of her time, including "illustrations" of the frescoes from the Villa of Mysteries in Pompeii, unearthed in 1910. Allison considered these frescoes fresh proof of her analysis of the poems. More recently, critics have dismissed her insistence on the primacy of the Mysteries; the poems are now read as a synthesis of Mystery and Apocrypha.

*

"Sweetest the Unexpected Sweet" can be read as part of the *Judith* narrative and also part of the annual Dionysian rite. It traces the first sexual intimacy between Judith and her maid. Within the Dionysian tradition, the maid is a eunuch. Many translations of this poem exist. The first canonical translation is now considered self-conscious and thus untrue to the original sense-content. The fragment I offer is the second translation that in 1982 became the accepted text. You may laugh at Judith's "doubt"; most readers do now. Even so, it does reflect the conservatism of the 1980s and the defensive and tentative American understanding of Eros. The 1982 "Sweet" was a better version, less self-conscious, and yet not anywhere near J II's vitality.

My contribution is the footnoted transliteration. I hope that it suggests a tone closer to the original polymorphous desire. I admit that it does sacrifice some vulgarity in the service of delight. That is my apology.

And yet there is no perfect translation of poetry, if poetry is difficult, and it is. Perfection, bah! My goal as a translator is not so much "perfection"—that ideal, that loss—as metamorphosis. Has the poem been transformed and transformed according to the spirit of the original? Is it still a baby alligator? Or is it only food now? A bird? From the perspective of the gods, metamorphosis remains finality, because you remain you to them, even as you fear you are not; you are food, the dead reptile, or the bird. The translator's hope is closer to the gods: hoping that whatever I change, whatever I choose to change, will not be changed essentially by my action. The translator's fear is where he falls back into the mortal realm: Fearing that the poem will never live on such a diminished understanding of its nature. In the end, the translator's dilemmas should fold back into the forgotten portals of secondary and debatable scholarship. What the reader wants to remember is not a process but a poem.

Prayer

O Lord, unto thee do I lift up my despicable heart,

      crawling with insects of tongue and hand,

crawling with the vermin of my every thought,

      crawling, Lord, like the lowest beast,

moaning with a wound that cannot be healed,

      cannot be helped, cannot close itself

but gapes open like a mouth filled with curses

      of blood and venom, bark and root.

O my tongue has lashed words like boats on a lake

      of fire, has driven the wild seas of my mind

to seize the horizon of Satan's glance, has lost

      all mooring in the storm of my heart's

delirium. He whom I love has taken my hands

      and made them wanton, made them want

the blood's boiling cauldron, made them seek out

      the night, delve into it like a miner digging

deep into the earth, seeking rifts of gold and emeralds

crusted into the sharp rocks, green

as the water of some fathomless sea, but finding only

the dank clay from which we all spring.

O Lord, but I loved the darkness, loved the spacious

underground caverns, swam in the cold waters,

dried myself in my lover's dark eyes, fed myself

on his voice like a serpent twining

around the neck of a motherless lamb. And he left me

here with burning words, empty hands,

left me naked, skin flayed with abandon, eyes seared

with the light of his skin. From thee, O Lord,

do I hide my despicable flesh. Free me from these shackles,

free me from the blood's fiery embrace,

take me from this hovel of sinew and bone to your bright

palace that I might find my voice

in the papery petals of Spring's most violet rain.

Gertrude of Brandenburg (d. 1502)

GERTRUDE OF BRANDENBURG died in a nunnery outside of Mantua, Italy, in 1502. Little is known about her life. It is thought that she might be the younger sister of Barbara of Brandenburg, the wife of Ludovico Gonzaga, the ruler of Mantua. It is known that Barbara had a sister Gertrude, but why and how she ended up in Italy is unknown. As the daughter of a wealthy Bavarian count, she would have most likely been married off to another provincial ruler, as was her sister. The fact that this poem was found in the papers of the Gonzaga family leads one to believe that she must have had a close connection with that family.

Translator's Note

I found this poem several years ago when I was doing research in Mantua, in the archives of the Gonzaga family, which ruled that city from 1328 to 1707. Actually, I was doing research on Andrea Mantegna, the court painter of Ludovico Gonzaga from 1459 to 1506. I was specifically interested in finding documents pertaining to Mantegna's wife, Nicolosia Bellini, the daughter of Jacopo and sister of Gentile and the great Giovanni Bellini. In my search, I came across some Italian translations of what I suppose are German or Latin originals of twelve prayers by Gertrude of Brandenburg, most probably younger sister of Barbara of Brandenburg, who was Ludivico Gonzaga's wife. I was able to find nothing more about Gertrude, except that she was born in 1452 and died in a nunnery in Mantua in 1502.

Whoever she was, Gertrude in these ten poems describes the spiritual journey of a woman who begins in an almost suicidal despair and ends in spiritual ecstasy. If she indeed was Barbara's sister, she was the daughter of the Markgraf Johann of Brandenburg and very well educated for a woman at that time, even one from a royal house. The poems reveal a passionate woman, first in physical abandon and then in an almost erotic fixation on God that is much like St. Teresa of Avila's. The translation I have included here is early in the sequence, perhaps the first or second poem.

One supposition is that Gertrude was visiting her sister in preparation to marry a neighboring ruler and became passionately involved with another man, who eventually spurned her. The poems are modeled on the Psalms but charged with the intense imagery and eroticism of the Song of Solomon. In my English translation, I have taken the language and cadences of the King James translation, which was undertaken a little over 100 years after Gertrude's death.

Olapa (Moon)

Give me a desk of Indian wood,
ink and a precious pen. Let me look behind
my dark eyes
and let me praise love for you.

The level open land appears in colors;
baked gritty ground, grass bristled fur, brush,
clouds and sky,
shapes of tall animals and their shadows.

I walk my open world bright amid its ashen colors
The spot of blood on the dry world's far horizon is you.
World so wide,
yet I live to know only you, and to know your shadow.

Give me a desk of any wood,
ink and a precious pen. Let me look in the night sky's
great bright eye
and let me fear my love for you.

KISARU GASHE (b.1955)

KISARU was born in 1955 and has composed poetry for most of his life. He was born among the Maasai on the Masai Mara game reserves of Kenya. Kisaru first gained attention when his verse won a pan-African poetry contest in 1984.

The Maasai are among the last people on the planet who have been living consistently in an ancient lifestyle from time immemorial. They speak a click language; the men herd cattle; the village is a circle of mud huts. The Maasai live on cow blood and milk. They wear brightly-colored blankets or sheets—plain or plaid, usually red—and lone individuals can be seen at great distances against the tan and green expanses. As a child, Kisaru learned Swahili and some English and French in a local elementary school; then a French family that had vacationed in Kenya for many years sponsored Kisaru's education abroad. Unlike many of those who leave, Kisaru came back, not only to Kenya, but to the Maasai lifestyle. He spends his days walking the vast landscape, carrying the short wooden stick his people use to nudge the cattle along. When the Maasai dance there is no knowing that one among their number is a poet, yet unlike those of his fellows, Kisaru's small hut is lined with poetry books. They are in English, French, and Swahili, but they are almost all by modern Africans.

Kenya's Poetry of Praise

I visited Kenya early in the summer of 2001 and met the Maasai poet Kisaru. A small group of Americans and Europeans were taken to a Maasai village and, because our guide knew I am a poet, I was brought to Kisaru and given an introduction. We spoke for a while, and again later, and he gave me poems. He wrote his first poems in Swahili, but said that even then he was mimicking the oral poetry that he had heard as a child, in recitations by the older people of his village. I asked if I could try to publish the poems he had given me and he said, "Olapa,"—the poem here. I have almost a book's worth of poems by Kisaru, but have only been given leave to share this one.

This poem was written in Swahili, but its title is in Maasai (sometimes called Maa). It begins with a paraphrase of a line that begins many epic poems in Swahili. The standard invocation is:

> Nipa loho ya kihindi
> wino na kalamu kandi
> nikuswifie mapendi.

> Give me a writing board of Indian wood,
> ink and a precious pen,
> let me praise love for you.

Kisaru's addition of "let me look behind my eyes," speaks to the fact that Swahili verse traditionally sounds aphoristic, but Kisaru and others have begun a trend toward the imaginative and descriptive.

As for the rest of the poem: driving through the Masai Mara feels vast, you go on forever under a huge blue sky, across endless tan and green. It's empty and then, now and again, you see a red speck on the horizon: humanity. (The Maasai explain that lions are afraid of red.) Kisaru brings all this into focus without mentioning a single color.

Kisaru says his influences are wide. The Nobel Prize-winning Nigerian playwright and poet Wole Soyinka has inspired Kisaru to write about living half in the world of traditional African spirits and half in the modern world. He also cites the verse of Nise Malange (a poet and activist, she translates other people's poetry from Zulu) and Sobonfu E. Somé (a lesbian poet who writes of gays and lesbians as "gatekeepers" in her tribal village: their sexual behavior is incidental, she says, what is noticed—and valued—is that they can help explain the men and women to each other). Nisa Malange's poem "I cry sing peace" catches the dangerous world "among the hippos and the soldiers." There is also the Ghanaian poet Ama Ata Aidoo who studied writing at Stanford, returned to serve as the Minister of Education in Ghana, and then went into exile in Zimbabwe with her daughter. Kisaru reports that what these poets have in common is that they build their permanent homes on boundary lines.

He speaks of particular affection for other Kenyan poets, the nineteenth-century pioneer of Swahili poetry Mwana Kupona binti Msham; the English-born Marjorie Oludhe Macgoye, who became a Kenyan citizen, and who writes that "changing continents in midstream/ is likely to create a mild upheaval:/ there is no need to lament loudly, like a woman/ chasing a runaway sheep in a tight skirt"; and Micere Githae Mugo, in exile in Zimbabwe.[1]

Kisaru Gashe is a very private person. The only photograph I have of him is from the back. A friend took a picture of me with a few of my Maasai friends and when I got home I saw that Kisaru had casually walked just behind our little group the moment the photograph was taken. It was clearly he, and I remembered that when I asked him to grant me a photograph, he had told me to look carefully at the pictures I already had.

Many Swahili words end in vowels, so, as is true when translating Italian, rhyme is sometimes difficult to avoid. I tried to capture the quietness in the poem, and did not match rhyme for rhyme. Kisaru told me when he writes it is often to a woman he has known most of his life. Sometimes, however, when he writes "you," it is the moon or the lion whom he is addressing. The Maasai coming-of-age ceremony for boys demands that the young man kill a lion. This is the only legal killing of lions that takes place on the Masai Mara. Kisaru said he has written to the lion he killed when he became a man, and also to the one that stole a child from his village when Kisaru was himself only a small boy. All this makes the poem a little scary, but somehow it creates a safe haven of itself. Here, love includes a hunger for the other's shadow, and so does fear, and so does the idea of writing.

---

[1] African Women's Poetry, Stella Chipasula and Frank Chipasula eds. (Heinemann: Oxford, 1995), 123.

Garrett Hongo as Casey Shigemitsu

Poem #10A

I grunt like an animal from Hell
While I hack and slash through the canes
And trample them under my boots.
But, evenings, when I hear the plaintive song of crickets,
I think to leave, just for them,
An island of stalks uncut and whispering
In the soft, tropical winds.

Poem #31

Bossman, there is gambling going on right under your nose,
And booze brewing out in the far fields,
Whores doing business by the mountain stream in Camp 9.
But you're laying stiff and alone in the dark,
And you can't put a shine on your nose, can you?
Pumping your hands, kissing the air…

Casey Shigemitsu (1885?–1958?)

CASEY SHIGEMITSU is the name scholars have given to the writer of *nikki*–journals in Japanese script—which survive from the time of the early sugar plantations on the North Shore of the island of O`ahu in the Hawaiian chain. His exact dates are unknown, but scholars estimate them to be between 1885 and 1958—spanning the time of the first immigration (the *kanyaku-imin*) through Roosevelt's "Gentleman's Agreement" early in the 20th century and two world wars. It is likely he was educated in Japan to a post-secondary level and briefly imprisoned by the Department of Justice during WW II. He lived in Kahuku, a sugar plantation town, and probably worked as a storekeeper for most of his life. Acting as an amateur folklorist, he roamed the canefields, collecting and transcribing field worker songs, known as *hore-hore bushi,* and preserved them in his journals.

THESE MARVELOUS POEMS came to me, out of an unchronicled history, by way of accident and fate. The Oral History Project at the University of Hawai`i-Manoa is their primary repository.

On a midsummer day some years ago, while sitting at one of the desks in the archives of the Project, I was listening to a collection of tapes of various interviewees who had been cane workers, storekeepers, and mill workers on the Waialua and Kahuku Sugar Plantations on the North Shore of the island of O`ahu—the very plantations where my ancestors had worked during the late 19th century and early part of the 20th. In the lengthy interview of a man named Roxas, a Filipino storekeeper from Waialua who was born in the 1920s, this storekeeper referred to songs Japanese cane workers would sing when he was a child. Roxas called them *huli-huli bushi*—work songs, except that *huli-huli* was Hawaiian for "winding" or "twisting," and the interviewer hadn't asked him to clarify that.

A few years after that, I heard a scholar speak at an Asian American Studies conference in Philadelphia. He presented a paper on *hore-hore bushi*, again Japanese work songs of the canefield laborers, but, this time, the man explained that *hore-hore* meant "work fast" in Japanese accented Hawaiian pidgin, that creole of English that eventually became the vernacular in Hawai`i. *Hore-hore* meant "hurry, hurry," you see. I thought back to the storekeeper Roxas, who, used to hearing all kinds of languages on the plantation, had simply transmogrified the words into Hawaiian—a quite natural change in his milieu. The song lyrics that the scholar quoted and then passed around in transcription and in English translation were powerful, stark, and raw—testimonials to tough labor and a record of both hope and resentment in those who worked the cane. But, to my mind anyway, they weren't quite poems.

Then, just a few months ago, came a call from Samuel Hiroshi Miyazawa, Joseph Lyons Professor of History at Claremont College, my alma mater. Sam is a third-generation Japanese American, an eminent scholar of the Tokugawa Period of Japanese History, and a friend from graduate school. He was very excited to tell me that he'd discovered something that he thought might interest me. He said that, the last time he'd been to O`ahu to see his family, he'd also stopped in at the Oral History Project to have lunch with Warren Kishi, the Director, who had been another classmate of ours. Warren told him of a new, as yet uncatalogued collection recently donated to the Project, a set of old storekeeper's journals and ledgers that they'd culled from several boxes of documents. They had been donated to the Project by a family in Waimalu on O`ahu, who'd found them in their garage while cleaning up. But these ledgers and journals were unusual in that, rather than the usual columns of profit and loss, inventory and sales, they contained daily narrative entries, kept by the storekeeper, in a running hand of the Japanese calligraphy style known as *sō-shyō*. Warren asked Sam if he might take a look at the stuff, Sam had immediately complied, and, after a few late afternoons buried in them, he'd been astonished to discover that what they amounted to was years of diaries the man had kept, recording daily events, ruminations, wishes, a flu epidemic, natural disasters, and labor conflicts during some twenty-odd years between 1919 and WWII, when the diaries stopped. In short, the diaries were a nearly complete history of the plantation generation of Japanese in Hawai`i.

Since then, as one of his personal scholarly projects, Sam had taken up the translation of these diaries. The author's name, though, had been quite difficult to determine, but he and Warren had assumed the man (as they assumed it to be a man, given that the diaries talked about a life as a plantation storekeeper—exclusively the occupation of men) to be a relative of the family who had donated the boxes of documents—a Sugiwara perhaps. But he wasn't. People whom the man quoted in his diaries as speaking to him called him "Shig" and "Casey," depending on whether they were pidgin- or English-speaking. And the Japanese addressed him as *sensei,* or "teacher," as it was known how educated he was, literate in written Japanese, a reader of esoteric books, a man who quoted poetry on occasion, who, for a small fee, would compose their letters home to loved ones in Japan, transcribed on a page of beautifully rendered calligraphy.

Sam was reading along in the diaries one day and was shocked to read the man addressed as "Shigemitsu." He remembered that it was the name of my mother's side of the family on O`ahu. He called because he wanted me to read what he'd translated so far—an unusually gracious offer, and, if I was agreeable, what he hoped was for me to help him render some of the poetry in the diary, for indeed, as in *Genji* and the Murasaki diaries, *The Pillow Book,* and scores of other works from the Medieval Period, there were short occasional poems and even longer, more narrative ones interspersed throughout the text. Some of them looked to be based on workers' songs and others on *katarimono*—narrative verses sung by traveling minstrels and reciters. The diarist writes of walking through the cane-fields, of transcribing workers' songs—the *hore-hore bushi,* his mundane life as a storekeeper, and learning the plots of Japanese silent movies—the *samurai* revenge-tragedies and the *shinjū* love suicides melodramas. There are descriptive passages of the village huts, worker clothing, cane trucks and the railroad, and women washing clothes. There is also a quite lengthy passage, perhaps fictional, about a love affair with a young woman who was fired from domestic work with the white planters but who refused to take up work in the fields, running off instead to Honolulu with a *benshi,* a traveling narrator of silent movies.

Shigemitsu, if it was actually the diarist's name, is indeed a family name of mine, and it was evident, after a while, that the man who wrote the diaries had been *detchi-boko,* a man who took the name of his wife's family after having married her and been adopted in. Usually, it was for the purpose of carrying on the name of a family who had no sons and who had land they could pass along to descendants. In the shopkeeper's case, however, there was no land to speak of as the Shigemitsu were plantation workers and owned nothing, and they had no lack of sons to continue the family name. Why he was *detchi-boko* seemed a mystery. And whom had he married? Was it one of my grandmother's sisters? It couldn't be my own grandmother, after all, as her husband was Kubota, my grandfather, who kept his own name and passed it down to my two uncles.

Regardless, though completely capable of doing the job himself, my friend Sam persuaded me to render the Japanese poems in the diaries into English. They are a mixture of elegance and rawness—raunchy as American blues in some poems, golden and sweet as Virgil's eclogues in others. The poet is a man born in Hawai`i at the beginning of the twentieth century, sent back to Japan as a youth for his education in a military school in Hiroshima, then repatriated back to Hawai`i just after WWI. He is about twenty when the diaries start, and he writes up until the day after Pearl Harbor in 1941 when he would be in his early 40s. He refers to himself variously, but, for the purposes of this anthology, I call him Casey *Shigemitsu* and suspect that it is the pseudonym of my own grandfather.

What I've included are two poems I believe based on plantation workers' songs. Like Allan Lomax, Shigemitsu was perhaps a folklorist as well as the author of a memoir.

Wayfarers

Wait, the wayworn
quavered. Away!
wailed the wayward,
undissuaded.
Always away!

We lay awake,
weighed "away"
and "wait" until
wait waned. Away
won.
Waverers
swayed, and then
still unpersuaded,
raced after us waving,
"Wait"—the way
we'd waited for.
Now eight days
along the way
into the wasteland,
our way's their way
and their way ours:
the way away.

Alan Lutiy (1899–1974)

ALAN LUTIY was, during World War II, a vigorous and vicious persecutor of Jews in Hungary's Gyor-Moson-Sopron region, which borders Austria. Sometime during the winter of 1944, then-Major Lutiy abandoned his post in the Hungarian Home Guard and made his way to what would become the American zone of Berlin, where he lived for four years in anonymity, working as a janitor and performing routine maintenance on apartment buildings, the same work he had done in his hometown of Gyor for twenty-five years before he joined the National Socialist party and began to move up the ranks. At the age of fifty, in Berlin, he apprenticed himself to a plumber. After five years, he became a licensed plumber, moved to Bonn and, benefiting from the West German construction boom of the fifties, made a dependable middle-class living.

During this time, he experienced a conversion that critics have likened, both ironically and with admiration, to St. Paul's on the road to Damascus. Lutiy's conversion, though, was self-induced. Working with an unspecified combination of hallucinogenic drugs, hypnosis, and yogic exercises, Lutiy seems to have wiped out his memory and awakened as a Jew. Many have suggested that the amnesia was more psychological than chemical. Others maintain stoutly that the amnesia was more opportunistic than chemical or psychological. For the rest of his life, Lutiy, who now called himself Zygmunt Cybulski, spoke, wrote, and responded to no language other than Polish, a language that he had evinced no facility in, or knowledge of, to that moment. He was, as far as anyone could actually detect from observation and interrogation, a Polish streetcar conductor from Zabrze who had survived the war by living in the forests until 1943, when he was captured and transported to the concentration camp at Lublin-Majdanek in eastern Poland. There is no record to substantiate Lutiy's claim. Lutiy, who would not respond to either his counsel or the prosecutor unless he was addressed as Herr Cybulski, was unperturbed when prosecutors pointed out that Zabrze has no streetcar line and that the area surrounding it is not heavily forested but dominated by mining and steel manufacturing. Lutiy proceeded to describe the layout of the streetcars, the details of every stop, the names and occupations of many of the regulars on his route, the other conductors, and his superiors until the judge ordered him to be silent. Later in the trial, though, he did observe wryly that if the allegations against him were true, that would explain the beatings that he received from his fellow prisoners at Lublin-Majdanek.

Lutiy was convicted of war crimes in 1957 and confined to the mental institution adjacent to Spandau. Though he would not normally have been sent to Spandau, which was restricted to German war criminals, prison authorities specially asked that he be confined there because qualified plumbers and pipe fitters were hard to come by during the heyday of the West German economic miracle. In prison, he had the freedom of the grounds as long as he had an authorized work order in his hands. And it was there, between 1957 and his death of cancer in 1974, that he turned to poetry, which of course he wrote in Polish.

A Note on the Text and Translation

The poems of Major Alan Lutiy (1898-1974) are notoriously difficult to translate, and even to obtain permission to attempt a translation has proved a burden that few scholars have been willing to assume. Because Lutiy thought of himself as a Jew, he left all his earthly goods, which consisted of a small library of books about pipefitting, a standard anthology of Polish poetry, and a manuscript of onionskin paper to the state of Israel. The sixty-seven poems that constitute his oeuvre were written on the backs of carbon copies of institutional work orders for plumbing repair, which are technically the property of the West German government.

Due to lack of interest, this theoretical conflict of property rights posed no problems until the poems were translated into German and published in *Todesspatz (Death Sparrow)*, a neo-Nazi underground journal that was distributed in Munich. Only one issue of the journal is known to exist. To this day, no one knows who the editors of *Todesspatz* were or how they came by copies of the poems, though technical aspects of the mimeographing (and some of the diction and spelling) suggest an American connection. There has been some speculation in scholarly journals that elements of the German-American communities in Cincinnati and Milwaukee might have been involved. This, however, is mere conjecture.

The publication of a neo-Nazi journal, illegal in Germany at that time as it is today, caused a stir in the press, though as far as investigators at the time could determine, only between nineteen and thirty-nine copies are known to have been left on doorsteps along the *Residenzstrasse* in Munich on June 23, 1979. Of those, at least six were rendered unreadable by a light mist that fell throughout the morning and into early afternoon. The German national archives contain only eleven confiscated copies of the edition, and of those, due to the vagaries of the mimeographing process and the limited proofreading skills of the editor or editors, only three have been deemed "complete" by scholars.

In the media storm that accompanied the distribution of inflammatory material along the *Residenzstrasse*—the street that Hitler took into the center of Munich after seizing the *Buergerbraeukeller* during his abortive "beer hall putsch" of 1923—the rights to Lutiy's manuscripts, which had sat untouched (except by whoever had made the original translation from Polish into German) in a cardboard box beside a boiler that Lutiy had tended for the last twenty years of his life, suddenly became important. By the terms of Lutiy's will, Israel owned the poems but did not possess the manuscripts. West Germany retained physical possession of the manuscripts but did not own the rights to the words—the "intellectual property"—on them. And those two claimants were soon joined by a third—a heretofore unknown daughter of Lutiy's claimed the same property rights that Israel claimed. She maintained—plausibly, it seems to me—that since her father was demonstrably and legally insane, he could not in sound mind have willed the rights to anyone, and that by the laws of inheritance those rights legally belonged to her.

I was able to secure the signatures of all three parties by promising each one-hundred percent of the proceeds. I will be able to honor that promise because the proceeds from poetry hover around the one number that can be divided into three equal one-hundred-percent piles and still total one-hundred percent: zero. Actually the final figure will come in considerably less than zero, if you count, as I must, all the chocolate and flowers I lavished on Fraulein Cybulski, as I was instructed to call her, for the better part of a year. No monetary figure can suggest the difficulties I encountered as I pursued the rights to these poems, though I am still angry that the accountants at my university have unreasonably disallowed the cost of two dinners, two breakfasts, and five bottles of champagne provided seriatim through the night by room service from the Trader Vic restaurant in Hotel Bayerischer Hof on the night of September 3, 1991. Those claims still seem to me necessary expenses that a poorly paid professor of German literature should not be expected to assume. Fraulein Bethlan found each and every one of those items essential before she could rouse herself "into a signing mood," as she put it. After she signed the waiver, I drove her to the airport for a noon flight to Milwaukee, for which I was also not reimbursed. As a result of all these machinations, I fell into such a lethargy that Xeroxes of the Lutiy material collected dust on my desk for almost a decade before I could force my mind to return to them.

The manuscript itself is organized alphabetically by sound. The first poem emphasizes the long A sound, the second the short A. The succeeding poems emphasize the B, C, D sounds, and are followed by poems in which the long E and then the short E are salient. When Lutiy had completed the alphabet, he moved onto poems that emphasized BA, CA, DA, etc. The poem I am republishing here foregrounds the WA sound, with a long A, in lines that have two beats per line, with iambics predominating. Some critics find the sound repetition mesmerizing, while others, perhaps the majority, consider it annoying. Over the fifteen years I have both worked on and avoided these poems, I have lived for long periods in both camps. At the moment, however, I have no opinion.

"Wayfarers" has been interpreted to combine the Anglo-Saxon poem known as "The Wayfarer" with the story of the Exodus, T. S. Eliot's "Wasteland," and more generally Kafka, though there is no evidence that Lutiy was familiar with those texts, or anything other than pipefitting manuals. Nothing in the poem bears the marks of the few texts scholars know for certain that Lutiy read, which I can attest to since I studied Lutiy's manuals thoroughly enough that I was able to re-plumb, to the standard prevalent in Germany in the mid-1960s, both the guest and master bath of the house my ex-wife now owns.

The poem has variously been interpreted as a Jewish poem celebrating the forty years the Israelites wandered in the Wilderness, an attack on the gullibility of the Israelites for parading in circles for forty years, a Nazi poem lauding the power of group identity, and a contemptuous dismissal of the Nazis who relinquished their individual identity to the group. I myself find all these alternatives equally compelling, though the poem is, at its base, indisputably an exercise in how many times Lutiy could employ the WA and A sounds in a poem and still cling to a modicum of sense.

Røma Kevnor Ainmo Ammom Rød Sered

Idlabinna Kevnor ilged aiv eht nwod gnirøjk
reis athtrea ta rerør i
enela ed retålrof ammom tgas nim
enennirt ges rednyks i ad go
ilocniv i orteip nas va nekrik va
mejh å remmok appap tgas nim reis enneh ta rerør i
negnagtdim egitir ned den ard rednev i da go
kkël ted rat rotkod tgas nim reis nuh
sesom solegnalehcim Kevnor
tkrets åsga tegem re gniksle sered nem å
regnittejk regnittejk regnittejks essid rof
enitselap i retep ts ednib etkurb rød mos
sslag rednu traveb Kevnor ges re go
nekrik emmas ned i tnis re sesom i rød
fkac nedlog rrd gnirkmo esnad rød mos
setilleaesi ttës Tarukkat
fkac nedlog gnirkmo esnad mos
dnåh gitkir snah dem ggejks snah nah rirv ån go
tof ertsnev snah va nellab lit kkev snah revyksrof go
enettelbatniens rerdams go po reppoh nah kils
med åp stnemdnammoc net dem.

Relle-gnag Tarukkat Tarukkat

ne tarukka tnis ta re gej

aseret ts sininreb mos

yelddid ob åap reknet gej esleyønrof arf tu eressap i

erbmettes aiv den yrrucs i mos

airottiv alled airam atnas va nekirk va enennirt liv po go

rutpluks euqorab rots sted dem

ås nenegleh åp eneelims moslegne mos i

retkis liprebblä snah Dnna

nrab te Tarukkat blä mos kkøs

nieb senneh mollem go blä blä

aseret ta åsgo tlatrof tkam drg i

gnirrmerfsgnindelggip va lim ekslegne ujsitrrf tåg

eitkcen ne rofegnals arboc ne kkåf

Tarukkat düh ekanselttar va tu tegal edisdaor

Kevnor devre suhtego telåmsrrps etsene ted

gilekriv idrof reksle de røjg ob.

Once Kevnor Went Where Everything Is Red

Little did Kevnor do in those days
but lie about and dream
of the great deeds our fathers had done,
how they fought the barbarians who came to slay
and were themselves slain,
when suddenly he heard his own father's voice
saying, "Take the boat and go!"
The sea was calm,
it didn't seem possible,
but Kevnor heard and obeyed;
he kissed Tarukkat and took the food she gave him.
As if by magic, the boat passed over
wave after wave
until he found himself in another world
where everything was red.
Kevnor looked at his hands: they were as red as farklefruit.
His clothes were red, as red as lobsters.
The water, red.
In terror he cried out for Tarukkat,
and as if in a dream he saw her floating
across the water, but she too was red!

Kevnor, Kevnor!
Pull at your oars, she cried,
but the water had turned to iron.
Set your sail, she cried,
but the sail blew away, rags in the wind.

Now eat the food I gave you, said she,

and Kevnor tore at her packet.

Blue berries spilled out, and he ate them,

and the water turned blue as minkelodion blossoms,

the sky, blue, blue as the eyes of Tarukkat,

and all else was as it should be.

I must remember this and tell the others,

said Kevnor, and began to pull for land.

Other fishermen were mending their nets,

and Tarukkat came waving and blowing kisses,

crying, Where have you been, Kevnor?

I will tell you, he said, but said nothing.

Kevnor (fl. early 19ᵗʰ C)

As far as is known, the poet Kevnor spent his entire life on the island of Edelskelluis, in the southern part of the Gulf of Bothnia, about forty miles from the Finnish coastal town of Uusikaupunki. In keeping with local usage, his full name was probably "Kevnor Kevnorsønne," though he would have been known only as "Kevnor" on an island small enough that a single name would suffice.

Kevnor's death and birth dates are uncertain, but occasional references in his work to mainland events (such as the annexation of Finland by Russia in 1809) make it possible to guess that he was born in the late 18th century and died some time before the middle of the19th.

Certainly it is clear from the poems that he was a fisherman, as were virtually all the men of Edelskelluis in that period. But there is more than one suggestion that he also made and at least attempted to sell nets; since other fishermen preferred to repair old equipment rather than buy new, Kevnor's enterprise appears to be an early attempt at entrepreneurship, one that evidently failed.

On Translating "Once Kevnor Went Where Everything Is Red"

Kevnor's first language was Dirja, a now-extinct tongue spoken only on Edelskelluis; what makes his work even more rare is that he is the only islander known to have written in that language. Dirja has many features in common with mainland languages of the region, with the notable exception of the hard-sounding "j" (thus "DEER-juh"). In selecting a poem to translate, I confess I was drawn to Dirja because it is a language rich in the letter with which my surname begins; indeed, another feature that sets Dirja apart from the languages of near-by countries is the frequency of words beginning with a double "k," as in "kkël" and "kkørs."

The last person to speak Dirja fluently was a woman named Kuoluüc Ndarot, who died in 1952 at the age of 76. Snatches of the language continue to be used in daily speech, though; for example, whereas Finnish is the language of ordinary usage, an islander might say in Dirja, "Dnuhtkaj, kkërt!" ("Move, hound!") to a dog, and the animals always seem to understand.

The only translation of Kevnor's poems—the only publication of any Dirja text, for that matter—is the Helicka and Kaminski edition published in Krakow in 1948. As I have no Polish, and as there are no published Dirja dictionaries or grammars, I despaired of being able to work in the language until chance led me to the International Bible Translation Centre in London in the fall of 2002, when I was living in that city. As is well known, Biblical translation has preserved many a dying language, though by the time I made my enquiry, I was reasonably certain that no work would have been done in Dirja.

But the Translation Centre staff directed me to Mr. Maurice Hargreave, who, as a young man, had rendered a good part of the New Testament into Dirja, ceasing at the death of Mrs. Ndarot. By visiting the island and speaking with her, he was able to compile a partial Dirja dictionary, which he very generously allowed me to photocopy. Long since retired from the Centre, Mr. Hargreave has returned to the Dirja translation that he put aside for so many years; there is no longer any point in printing Bibles in Dirja since the language is extinct, but Mr. Hargreave pointed out to me that his time is his own these days and referred to "a constitutional inability to leave any task unfinished," apparently even one that has lain idle for a half century. A recent bout of extended ill health has slowed his progress, but he expects to finish the Gospel of Luke within the next two years and move on to the Gospel of John.

In translating "Once Kevnor Went Where Everything is Red," I have relied on Mr. Hargreave's dictionary, on information gained from his kind answers to my many questions, and, regrettably but necessarily, on sheer guesswork. The reader will notice that I have punctuated where Kevnor did not; it seemed the thing to do if the poem's full drama were to emerge. One seeming typo should be explained: in line 8 of the second stanza, the two-word phrase "blue berries" is used, but that is because "liprebblä," literally "blueberries" in Dirja, probably refers to a fruit more like lingonberries than the domestic blueberries *(Vaccinium angustifolium)* that Americans put on their breakfast cereal.

Thematically and structurally, the poem is, except for its obvious brevity, not unlike other seafarers' tales; there is the journey, the crisis, the summoning of magical powers, and the rescue, though not without a price. In the fourth-to-last line, there appears what may be taken as a sly dig at the fishermen who would rather mend their old nets than buy a new one from Kevnor. His (or his persona's) baffling refusal to tell his story sounds like the mythic traveler's traditional inability to recount his adventures to an audience that has no basis for understanding them. More pertinent to the fate of Dirja, it is almost as though the speaker falls silent in the eerie foreknowledge that, one day, the language itself will no longer be heard.

I continue to work on Kevnor's poetry in the hope that my renderings will become more and more precise as Mr. Hargreave's study of Dirja continues. All errors in the present translation are, of course, my own.

Inge, in Rehab

It hurts at first
sticking fingers down your throat.
Vomiting's an art
but after years of practice
I can do it now
just by thinking about it
the way some women can come
reading a sexy book.
It's like I open a door
and walk into a place that's mine
a place where I can look at
my knobby spine in the mirror
my breasts a guy I used to date
called little bee stings.
I haven't bled since I was sixteen.

I shoplift, too.
I don't know why I do it-—
usually groceries
but sometimes jewelry
bathing suits and shoes.
I walk right out in anything
I like. The social worker

they make me see in here
says it's part of the same disease:
taking and putting back.
She tells me I need to
learn to love myself
but it's too late for that.
She tells me I need to
meditate, take up a hobby

but I already have one.
As soon as they let me out
I will eat till I overflow.
I will cram it in, 2 quarts
of Häagen Dasz, 2 bags
of chips, handfuls of candy bars
and then I will throw it up
in Anglo-Saxon. I will puke.
I will barf like a dog who's gorged
on carrion, then fills his gut with grass.
A dog who heaves it up, then trots
back to the deer carcass.

Greta Schoenemann-Licht (b. 1948)

GRETA SCHOENEMANN-LICHT, an only child, was born in Berlin, Germany, in 1948. Her father had been a minor Nazi functionary who narrowly escaped a prison sentence in the aftermath of the war, her mother an elementary-school teacher. They lived in the Russian sector of the city. Greta remembers her childhood as a constricted period; there was barely money for food and heat. Old friends of her parents were suspect and new friends hard to attain. Her mother initially lost her position but was reinstated. Her embittered father never found employment again.

Schoenemann-Licht was just entering adolescence when the so-called Berlin Crisis of 1958 began. The next four years of arguments between the Americans and the Russians, including the all-but-fruitless Krushchev-Eisenhower dialogue at Camp David, the building of the Wall, a tank confrontation at Checkpoint Charlie in October of 1961 that very nearly led to an exchange of gunfire, all colored her girlhood. She began to write poetry during this fraught period and continued while at the Freie Universitaet in Berlin. Now a psychiatric social worker and single mother, Schoenemann-Licht lives with her two grown children in Charlottenburg. Her first book of poems, *Hilfe kommt (Help Is Coming),* was published in 1998. She is the author also of several monographs in her field and co-editor of a textbook on psychosocial disorders.

On Schoenemann-Licht and Her Poem

It is not surprising to find psychiatric social worker Greta Schoenemann-Licht taking as her subject dysfunctional young women whom she has met and treated over the past twenty-five years. Married to an international law professor with whom she had two children, subsequently divorced, Schoenemann-Licht returned to university to study for her multiple degrees in psychology, social work, and comparative literature. She credits her ex-husband, with whom she has remained on amicable terms, with providing both the financial and moral support that made it possible for her to study for these advanced degrees and for attentive parental support of their daughters.

"Inge, in Rehab" is one of a series of dramatic monologues this poet has undertaken, inspired by patients she has encountered in her practice. While she does not specialize in the treatment of adolescents, she confesses that they interest her the most. I met with her in Manhattan while she was attending a symposium on psychosocial disorders, and had the good fortune to interview her. In our question and answer exchange published this year in *The East Coast Review of the Arts,* she replied to my question about her choice of subjects: "It's because they are still in their formative years. Intervention has its greatest chance of success at this vulnerable period. Also, I feel quite empathic with them; I grew up in the bad times when the Wall loomed over us, another war threatened, and we were still leading lives of deprivation and anxiety. And that, after all, is what these kids are feeling. They may be living in what you Americans call 'the lap of luxury,' but internally what they feel is deprivation, is anxiety."

The character, Inge, appears sullen, bitter, unrepentant, in the grip of her bulimic urges. Schoenemann-Licht remembers experiencing much the opposite in terms of extremes. There was barely enough food on the table. Portions were judiciously meted out, leftovers were closely guarded. Even if the desire to do so existed, there was nothing in the shops to shoplift. But it requires only a small leap of imagination for her to enter into her character and speak in her voice. We see this illness in full bloom. This episode in the rehabilitation unit will, we infer, be only the first of a series before Inge can come to grips with her desperate need to gorge on food and then purge. At the moment, all she can do is fling her story before the reader.

The voice in this monologue is deliberately arrogant, tough, and alive with self-hate. The use of enjambments—"She tells me I need to/..." "She tells me I need to...." points up the irony of these glib words of advice. The final tropes for vomiting, "I will throw it up/ in Anglo-Saxon, I will puke./ I will barf...," certainly indicate how fluent Schoenemann-Licht is in contemporary American slang. This she credits to several of her patients, all of whom have studied English from the early grades on. They are "kids desperate to out-American Americans," as she puts it.

Everything about this poem invites the reader to move on to the poet's later monologues, "Magda of Hospice House," about a determined young Romanian who crossed the Danube in 1989 to begin a new life in the West, and "The Mindhunter," the study of an obsessive-compulsive middle-aged man who formerly investigated obsessive compulsive murders for the FBI. These are part of a new manuscript seeking a publisher.

A lively, inquiring mind informs *Hilfe kommt, (Help Is Coming);* it introduces a mature voice that has not been heard until recently and deserves attention from psychologists and poetry readers alike.

Ululations of Late

A sting on brass.
A thought tingles
on a face,
lights its candles.
Then the masses…
Showooosh
Showiiissshsh…
On
polished floors…
in the atom's bureaucracies…
the sun as usual
screaming inside her
glass
cage.

Shotgun blasts.
The bride deflowered.
A twenty one gun salute,
Marshal Tito again.
A gargling
tearing
the Adam's apples

of rubbery throats.
Wet, wet the broken
water main,
the silver wheat of
Bffsssssssst Shffsssssst
splashing on
the road.

TAFIDA ZEINHUM (1924–1989)

TAFIDA ZEINHUM was born in Tanta, Egypt, in 1924. She was raised in a land-owning family; as happened in many such cases among the Egyptian gentry, her father married a second wife who was urban and educated. Showing great promise in school, Zeinhum went to Cairo, where her father enrolled her in the prestigious Ramses school. At the second wife's insistence, Zeinhum was ultimately allowed to enroll at Cairo University in 1940.

Before and during WWII Egyptian politicians called for independence; Egyptian feminists went about Cairo condemning the use of the hijab, promoting family planning, condemning polygamy, and initiating literacy programs for women. Labor movements were on the rise as the country became more industrialized. Zeinhum, again with the encouragement of her father's second wife, participated in these activities and found herself drawn to socialist and communist circles. There she met and fell in love with the novelist Abbas Khashaba, who went on to become head of Egyptian radio and television during Nasser's reign. They were married in 1947, and divorced ten years later.

An avid reader from her youth, Zeinhum began corresponding with children's magazines and published her earliest writings there, and in her teens won a national youth poetry contest. This was a time of socialist realism and nationalist romanticism, and Zeinhum wrote within those veins. However, it was her encounter with Widn wi Talat Manakhir (Three Noses One Ear) and the writings of an iconoclastic group of experimental writers influenced by surrealism (led by Georges Henein, Ramses Younan and Fouad Kamel) that attracted her attention. In an article about the group in *Rose al-Youssef*, she wrote, "it is this kind of writing that most exemplifies our condition and its contradictions, a society where all ages of human history coexist side by side, and not in harmony."

Zeinhum's reputation began to rise in the late 1970s through the work of young feminist scholars, and with the emergence of the 1970s poets who openly championed her in their clandestine journal *Adhwa 77 (Lights 77)*. Three decades after her expulsion in the 1950s for advocating feminist and revolutionary principles, she was reinstated in the Egyptian Writers Union in 1983 in a ceremony attended by Naguib Mahfouz, Tawfiq al-Hakim, and most of her former detractors. Sharqiyat Press published her collected poems in 1987. She died in 1989 of natural causes. Recent memoirs of various Egyptian writers have revealed that she and her Japanese lover of many years provided refuge for several communist, and even Muslim Brotherhood, intellectuals whom the Nasser government began persecuting and torturing in the 1960s.

I CAME ACROSS ZEINHUM'S NAME in Abdelqaher al-Janabi's book on Arab surrealists, *Shayatin Makhboula: Aan al-Soryalia fi al-Adab al-Arabi al-Hadith (Perverse Imps: On Surrealism in Modern Arab Literature),* one of the few works on the subject, the title of which comes from a letter by Andre Breton sent to Henein in which Breton wrote, "The imp of the perverse, as he deigns to appear to me, seems to have one wing here, the other in Egypt." Zeinhum, according to Janabi, a rather orthodox surrealist, was a minor figure in the movement. In an interview, Zeinhum reported that she came across the notion of automatic writing through her contact with Kamel, who was also a talented painter. Some of her earliest writings exhibited the influence of the visual arts and Cubism in particular, even though she later revised some of those writings into rhymed metrical verse "to enhance their surrealist effect."

By the early fifties Zeinhum began to disagree openly with the Surrealists about the influence of dreams and argued that art, and poetry, need to be "constructed dreams," that the conscious mind should seek to consciously invert reality, and must attempt to create a contrarian reality which will help unveil the nightmarish nature of our lived experiences. She wrote in a 1951 essay, "By our lived reality, I do not mean a cosmic, ahistorical concept, or some sense of a tragic nature of humanity. We must begin with the real, and start consciously dressing the real with the masks that fit it. We create metaphors, but I would hasten to add that these masks of the real must be porous enough that we see the skin of reality under them, and however we distort the shape of the veritable's head, we need to maintain some of its features. That's what the dream world can help us achieve."

A thorough secularist, Zeinhum conceded to her critics that such strategic plunges into the imaginary may not lend the wide revelations the imagination is capable of rendering available to us. However, she added, "the dream world does not have a methodology of its own knowledge; it does not have a method of arranging information. The dream world is a mad magician's garage."

Encouraged by Surrealist rebuttals, Zeinhum decided to reattempt automatic writing, but not with her writing hand. In 1952 she began to exclusively write poems using her left hand. In the aforementioned interview she explained, "I don't want to catch everything the imagination gives. I want to catch only what is significant. My right hand is greedy; it wants everything. My left hand is too slow and will use its faculties to catch only the interesting things that the mad magician we call the dream world throws at us."

The poem "Ululations of Late" was written in 1966. In many ways it is reminiscent of some of Robert Creeley's early work, such as his famous poem "I Know a Man," particularly the last stanza when so much happens so quickly. In Creeley's poem his montage technique is most evident, cutting a great deal of narrative and pasting bits of scenes to one another whereby the poem lurches, and where the reader experiences a kind of jet-lag, a wooziness due to lost time, but remains very much in the world of the poem. Of course, the energy of Zeinhum's poem, where a great deal of action is presented only to have the poet deny us arrival, is a kind of inverse of Creeley's practice.

In my own practice, I find it difficult to tackle and shake my readers, probably due to the fact that in my American voice, my sense of the lyric depends on that voice's insecurity, however genuine that insecurity may be. This tenuousness constitutes the American poets' major contribution to the American psyche, an affirmation of our isolation and the reader's. In Zeinhum's practice, she makes the startling image and the jigsaw puzzle-nature of her assembly the major reward and most prominent aspect of the poem. In this poem where much focus is devoted to sound, the oral images and the visual vie for the reader's attention at the expense of one another, which affirms Zeinhum's claim that "the senses are never in harmony. To bring them together is art's dreamy occupation."

Defenestration

your mother leaps from a chic hotel
with a whooshing sound, a wishing.
the sweet perfume of the lily in her hair
parts the night sky with a kissing.

oh, you could make believe anyone loved you
now that the anchor has been pulled
from the coraline bottom of a glassy sea
called *mere mer* or *murmur* or *hold.*

you shouldn't wonder if god smiles now
from his picklejar heaven inside the bar
in the swank hotel where you sit and sip
miraculous oceans of gin. you are

after all, the shattered glass caught
in a palm that pours you another shot.

Fora da janela

Sua mãe salta de um hotel chic com um som
como o vento. Aquele é o que você deseja. O
perfume doce do lírio em seu cabelo
parte o céu da noite com um beijo.

O, você poderia fazer para acreditar
qualquer um amou-o agora que essa escora
estêve puxada do recife de um mar
de vidro chamado *mere mer* ou *murmur* ou *da*

preensão. Você não deve querer saber se o deus
sorrir agora de seu paradise da bacia dos peixes
dentro da barra no hotel do extravagante onde você
se senta e bebe o miracle dos oceanos do whisky.

Você é, apesar de tudo, o vidro quebrado travou
em uma palma que o derramasse que outra disparou.

João Pudim (1917–1963)

João Pudim was one of the great heartthrobs of Brazil. A gifted poet and musician, Pudim revolutionized the jazz world with the invention of *bossa médio,* which departed radically from the earlier *bossa velho* and which set the stage for the *bossa nova,* which became an international sensation. Pudim received Brazil's prestigious *Macaco Durado* Award in 1947 for his collection *Sonnets do Português.* Only thirty years old at the time of the award, Pudim received major critical attention. It was to be his downfall. He didn't produce another volume for thirteen years, during which time he declined in health due to chronic alcohol and opium use. He also sustained a major head injury caused by a falling *ourico,* the large seed-bearing pods of the Brazil nut tree. His subsequent collection, *minha cabeça é ferida,* though technically brilliant, was nearly incomprehensible. It was panned in the press, and Pudim slipped into obscurity. He died at the age of forty-five from an abscessed bowel, caused partially by his drinking and partially by his habit of swallowing dressmaker's pins (he said they provided him with necessary nutrients such as iron and manganese). His final volume, *Tempestade Mortal,* appeared posthumously, garnering major attention and a new, younger readership who had grown weary of Portuguese syntax. Banners in the streets proclaimed *"Nós odiamos a sintaxe; viva Pudim"* or "Down with Syntax; Long live Pudim."

Why Defenestration?

I chose to translate Pudim partially because of his extraordinary work and partially because of my love of Brazilian music. Pudim straddles both the world of poetry and the world of jazz; his poems have a vibrant, modern, syncopated feel. They reach after the odd turn of phrase, the jarring image, with a sort of improvisatory feel. One cannot but think of the saxophone as a suitable correlative to his quick turns of wit and flashes of various tones. Indeed Pudim's music is often performed on sax (though he himself played the euphonium and slide trombone).

"Defenestration" is an early poem; it deals in part with his uneasy relationship to tradition as well as the alienation he felt from his family (farmers and cab drivers, they never understood his artistic ambitions; his mother urged him repeatedly to join the army or to pass a civil service exam so that he might gain a respectable position as a government official). His agnosticism (later recanted) is evident in the lines where he posits god as living in a fishbowl in the bar (I've translated it as "picklejar" for obvious reasons). And certainly the substance abuse that would plague him the rest of his days was anticipated in the poem's setting.

This is perhaps one of the best examples of Pudim's mastery of traditional form, yet it still has about it a looseness, a playfulness of both sound and form. One can see in these lines the beginnings of his fragmentary and elliptical lines, as he allowed the surface of his poems to crack and disjoint. His experiments in poetry anticipate the efforts of writers as diverse as Anne-Marie Albiach and Roger McGough, as well as the lyrics of maestro Antonio Carlos-Jobim, best known for such hits as "One Note Samba" and "Song of the Jet."

A few additional notes on the translation: I'm indebted to Willis Barnstone and his volume *The Selected Pudim* (Banana Editions, 1972), which first brought Pudim's work to my attention. I actually found a copy of the bound galleys at Aardvark Books in San Francisco; someone had laboriously blacked out all references to nuts, perhaps as some cryptic homage to Pudim pre-accident. Frankly, I had no idea what had been blacked out (so thoroughly was the deed done) until I spoke with Barnstone at a conference in Chicago. He generously sat with me at the bar of the Michigan Avenue Hilton, through round after round of badly watered-down gimlets, and restored all of the missing nut references.

As I don't speak Portuguese that well, I've taken a few liberties with idiomatic usages. Hopefully, those will either be apparent and forgivable or they'll slip by unnoticed. Either way, I tried at least to stay true to Pudim's playful spirit and his sardonic sense of humor.

It is my express hope that more will be written on Pudim and that more writers will discover this jewel of the Amazon basin. In his own words, *"a prova de um homem não é por como é falado aproximadamente, mas por quem* (the proof of a man is not how he is spoken about, but by whom)."

A Corpse Should Be Breathless

Something's wrong in the coffin. Pull out the nails.
Who would take a bride so shady?
Please, mister. Think hard.

Such a big girl, yes, very big. A lady ghost.
The moon will hide beyond the sky—frightened.
Something's wrong in the coffin.

A corpse must be breathless, a lump in the throat.
Take it back to the mortuary—take it like candies.
Please, mister. Think hard.

There are corpses and dead bodies.
There are always women—Yellow paper, red brush, black ink,
wooden sword. Something's wrong in the coffin.

Cover it up, hurry! It's enough to make me choke.
Put incense on the grave, so it's an omen.
Don't be scared. Please, mister, think hard.

This one is turning—and look at you, so frightened.
Can't you stop turning into a walking corpse?
Something is wrong in the coffin.
Think hard, please. Mister?

WEN BO (1817–1891?)

WEN BO grew up in the village of Shi-Ju on the island of Hong Kong. Although his work is scarcely known outside of his native land, he has been influential not only with that group of poets who would revive the medieval tz'u poetic form, but with certain directors of the popular Hong Kong cinematic movement as well. What little fame he has outside Hong Kong is the result of his participation in London's Hester Street Movement, a loose affiliation of radical, anti-imperialist poets active at the end of the 19th century. Although a number of his poems are available in their original Cantonese, they have been translated into English only once before, by Duncan Rose in the chapbook *Sixteen Poems for a Dying Land* (Muse Press, 1890). Wen Bo died in London, probably in December, 1891.

On Wen Bo

Often, when I relax in my study to consider Hong Kong, my mind drifts back not to the heady time of that grand island's return to Chinese rule, but much earlier, to the gentler years just before the first Opium War. Who, walking through those dusty portside streets, could have predicted the role Hong Kong would play not only in Britain's grand colonial theatre, but in the tragic fall of traditional China as well? The Hong Kong of the early nineteenth century was but a cluster of villages, ringed by a meandering coastline, inlets, and coves, ideal hideouts for the many pirates who preyed upon passing merchant ships. In retrospect, the island takes on a romantic cast, the sun slipping easily behind Victoria Peak, fishermen taking in their nets, a pall of morning fog sweeping over the low thatch huts. For the Hong Kong of the slow years before the Opium Wars made its meager living not through warships and blood, but through the gentler trades of incense shipping (after which the island is named), trawling, and the hard work of the many farmers who tilled the fertile land.

It was on just such a now-vanished farm, halfway up the many-tiered Victoria Peak, that Wen Bo (1817-1891?) composed his first awkward poems. Described by those who knew him as a lanky, wan, ungainly young man, he walked with a limp, working his father's farm during the day and composing late into the night. Of course he was an eccentric—all great poets are eccentrics—and his *ouevre* is slim, for though he lived a very long life, he abandoned his art when he was not quite forty years old, turning his attentions to the politics of rebellion instead. Because he believed poetry—especially the florid, romantic verse popular in his day—impotent in the face of great economic and political turmoil, he put down his brush in favor of the sword. He appears to have participated abortedly in the second Opium War (1856-1860), then, later, in the Taiping Rebellion, where he worked as a kind of accountant and, should rumor be taken for fact, a spy.

Here, he disappears from literary history, only to resurface briefly in London, under the name of William Bo, where he appears to have found employment as barkeep of the Finger Bone Pub. Although his position with the anti-imperialist avant-garde of Hester Street is sketchy, it was during this time that his early work was first published outside of China, in a five-penny chapbook edition by the radical Muse Press, edited and translated by Duncan Rose, that inestimable promoter of foreign writers. (Wen Bo's original Cantonese manuscripts, dating from the time of the poems' composition, are available for perusal by special appointment in the Reading Room of the British Museum.)

I first came upon *Sixteen Poems for a Dying Land* at Cecil Court Books, a small antiquarian bookstore near London's theatre district. I was initially attracted not to the poems, but to the odd inscription on the inside cover from the famous Duncan Rose to Wen Bo himself. "For my dearest friend, Wen Bo," the delicate inscription reads, "and to our vampiric future together." Like most Victorian-era chapbooks, this one contained no biographical note. Nor did the poems, printed on cheap, yellowed paper, appear in their original language. And, truth be told, the translations offered by the Muse Press were florid in the extreme, filled with the "thee's" and "thou's," the sweeping gestures, the literary pretensions of the worst of the Hester Street Society's work. It was only on a closer examination that I sensed the art of a great poet concealed beneath the cheap wool blanket of Rose's translations. And what did that odd inscription mean?

Needless to say, it is through a great deal of scholarly work both in London and at the Chinese University of Hong Kong that I've been able to bring Wen Bo's work justly to light. Wen Bo was something of a reactionary writer, and, thus, an odd choice for Muse Press and Duncan Rose, who considered himself at the very vanguard of the liberal thinkers of the day. No doubt it was Wen Bo's own biography that drew Mr. Rose to his work, and not the poems themselves, which are carefully composed in the tz'u style of Chinese poetry. Tz'u poetry, a medieval form which holds to a strict pattern of rhyme and tonal repetition, was originally sung to popular court melodies, though Su T'ung Po, the 11th-century innovator of the style, introduced tz'u poems liberated from the constraints of melody, a style that exerts the strongest influence on Wen Bo's own work.

In my translation of "A Corpse Should Be Breathless," I have eschewed the romantic bluster of the Rose translations in favor of preserving something of the formal elements of the poem. And, since tz'u poetry is quite alien to readers of English poetry, I have opted for the villanelle, a more familiar medieval troubadour form, as the best vehicle for Wen Bo's poem. If I have taken any liberties with the sense of the poem in favor of preserving its formal conceits, I beg the reader's forgiveness.

Although the circumstance of the poem is quite clear, it might help the reader to know something of the subject's context. "A Corpse Should Be Breathless" deals with that figure of popular Chinese mythology known as the hopping corpse (or *Jiangshi*). The hopping corpse—an angry corpse whose soul (or *po*) has not yet left its body—lies eternally awake in the coffin. As *rigor mortis* sets in, the corpse can no longer walk, so when released he hops from place to place looking for a solution to whatever has him unsatisfied—proper funeral oblations perhaps, or a better burial plot. When the hopping corpse encounters the living, he strangles him or, in some cases, bites his neck, thereby draining his blood. For this reason the hopping corpse is often called the Chinese vampire and is doubtless that thing alluded to in Mr. Rose's inscription. What the hopping corpse represents in Wen Bo's poem—the death of old Hong Kong, the peculiar conscience of the speaker—is up to the reader to determine.

To me, it seems high time that Wen Bo's work—particularly those poems he wrote just before his renunciation of poetry—came to American and British audiences. I hope it will serve as a kind of tonic for that brand of Larkinesque irony, that coyness, that winking wit and prosaic style so common in the works of the youngest generation of English language poets, for Wen Bo's poetry is appealingly direct, earnest, lyrical and, most of all, unafraid of sentiment.

It might serve as an interesting postscript for readers to know that Wen Bo's work, while obscure in *all* parts of the world, has not escaped the notice of a small band of devotees of 19th-century Hong Kong poetry. One of them, Chuek-Hon Szeto, has even directed a popular film—*Mr. Vampire*—on the subject. Almost every line of "A Corpse Should Be Breathless" is alluded to in that classic of Hong Kong cinema.

And This He Said

And this he said: Hail, thou art exalted… [Hail] thou art adored …

…Bequeathed [betrothed] ……… soul in heaven, bone on earth

And this he said: ……… between your limbs…… Tender of Gardens, Mother

…… a son will be ……… who is the sun………[1]

And this he said: through your loins all becoming will come… …

Harmonies of blood……… durations of eternity…

And this he said: … each year spelt yellows then greens anew……

Thou art chosen……… green greener than the great inundation[2]

And this he said: [as] ……… Ka[3] seethes into thee … open your mouth

Warm your mortar for the pestle of this seed[4]

And so for me was he desirous

And so he spoke but was denied

---

[1] A conflation of Horus the Elder, a solar deity, and Horus, the son of Isis and Osiris.
[2] The annual inundation of the Nile.
[3] Spirit and life force of humans and gods.
[4] Conception was thought to be possible through the mouth as well as the vagina, and the vagina was considered a mortar.

For this I, Hekenus, said: I've not finished braiding my hair, kohling my eyes
I've just cut the curled sidelock from my brow[5]

For this I, Hekenus, said: dates I've picked await.... [their eating]..............
...I......... advent and abandonment......

For this I, Hekenus, said: meantime meanwhile... [as all] existing
.... to bake [bread], to spin, to weave, to carve my name

For this I, Hekenus, said: I've yet... [becoming]........ let me become
Not precedent or augury...... me......... aftermath in afterglow

For this I, Hekenus, said: summer hours are long... myrrh [perfumes]...
My...[people]...... laid waste;[6] wild geese soar in a craze of flight

For this I, Hekenus, said: fields are rampant with corn, with sugar cane and cotton,
I will be grinding girl, driver of chariots, priestess, hairdresser, supervisor of the
    cloth

For this I, Hekenus, said: I will be treasurer, steward, composer, mourner, musician
weaver, dancer, designer of wigs, choreographer of pleasures for the king[7]

For this I, Hekenus, said: I will not enter the plot of your desire to make me
    legible to the ages
nor........ wear a false beard or male garb to steal away[8]

---

[5] A curled sidelock was a symbol of childhood.
[6] This probably refers to the stele of the pharaoh Merneptah in which a people named Israel are "laid waste," up to now the only extant non-Biblical documentation of the existence of Israel.
[7] This is a litany of many of the occupations available to women in ancient Egypt.
[8] A reference to Queen Hatshepsut, who declared herself Pharaoh and often wore male clothing.

For this I, Hekenus, said: before *Khamsin*[9] drives dust ………
30 ……….. parched soil cracks again … ……

For this I, Hekenus, said: Numbered as the flies……… could not be counted up[10]
………[like] bulrushes toppled by scythes

For this I, Hekenus, said: ……… useless to seek……… lamentations save
  [no]………
[I] follow my heart and its happiness, seize day and night, the very air burning[11]

35 For this I, Hekenus, said: I will wear woven garlands around my throat,
Pin lotus to my hair, bathe Nileside ……… eyes……… stones of the great light[12]

For this I, Hekenus, said: your mysteries are not welcome
My mysteries I wield but will not yield

And so to me, tender of gardens, made he tender
40 And so by me was he denied.

---

[9] A fierce hot wind known to blow for fifty days.
[10] This refers again to the text of the stele of Merneptah.
[11] Hekenus's desire to seize the day seems closer to an Israelite's way of thinking than to that of most Egyptians, who looked forward to an afterlife.
[12] "Stones of the great light" probably refers to diamonds, suggesting that Hekenus will bathe at night, under the stars, very likely a daring act on her part.

HEKENUS (fl.12ᵗʰ c B.C.)

HEKENUS was an Egyptian poet who, it is safe to say, wrote "And This He Said" in the middle of the 12th century B.C., during the great age of love poetry. Though only 5% of the Egyptian population were literate, and the percentage of women who could read and write was, no doubt, considerably less than that, it is quite possible that Hekenus transcribed her own work. It is, of course, also possible a scribe wrote her verses down for her. Since she so pointedly announces her name in each couplet she speaks, I would venture a guess that Hekenus was someone of note in the society—perhaps the Hekenus of the Hekenus and Iti duo of well known musicians of the time. I would guess, too, that she was either an Israelite who had been sold as a slave into Egypt or an Israelite who had crossed the border from Canaan into Egypt in order to escape famine (there is abundant evidence of such emigrations because of the fertility guaranteed by the annual Nile inundation). It seems more than likely, by virtue of the confident tone of her poem, that Hekenus, like the Biblical Joseph, somehow became assimilated into Egyptian society and made her way up the social ladder. To be sure, I have little more than the strength of her voice and the references she makes to rely on, but, having lived with Hekenus and her poem for some time, I have come to believe that my hypothesis is, in this case, very close to the truth.

"AND THIS HE SAID" is a remarkable document that came into my hands a number of years ago when I visited Egypt and had the good fortune to meet a professor of ancient Egyptian literature who proposed that I do an English translation of the poem.

By the late 20th century, the basics of the ancient Egyptian language—vocabulary, word order, sentence patterns—had been established, and scholars were avidly working on the texts and formal structures of an extensive Egyptian literature that had survived as many as five millennia, most of it predating what we had come to think of as the earliest writings of humankind—the Bible and the great works of Greece and Rome.

Ancient Egyptian literature was almost exclusively a verse literature. That includes "wisdom" texts, laments, prayers and hymns, and most of the tales, to say nothing of the considerable body of love poetry that has come down to us.

Much of this poetry was written in couplets—thought couplets, they're called—which made up complete verse sentences. In addition, with the exception of enjambment and rhyme, ancient Egyptian poets had availed themselves of many poetic devices, from metaphor to imagery to word play. Repetition and parallelism were pervasive. All was of great interest to me, especially since received forms, word play, and repetition have always been staples of my own poetic practice. And so, with the professor's literal transcription in hand, I embarked on my first venture at translating a "text" into the "poem" I could only hope it was intended to be.

Hekenus, the author of, and, I believe, the speaker in, "And This He Said," was a woman, and a mighty feisty, determined one at that. I liked her immediately. First, her words offered ample evidence that feminism was not simply a 20th-century phenomenon of Western origin, and second, she was a true original, since almost all extant ancient Egyptian texts are believed to have been written by men. Furthermore, the poem I was to translate, predating Christianity by at least 1200 years, seemed to be an account of an Annunciation described by the "chosen" woman herself—a woman who, astonishingly, responds to the offer made to her with a resounding NO.

There is a considerable body of evidence that women in ancient Egypt enjoyed extraordinary rights—rights unequalled in any other part of the ancient world, rights equaled in many places only in the last century, and rights, sad to say, still unknown in many parts of the globe. Indeed, Herodotus believed that the Egyptians had "reversed the ordinary practices of mankind" because women could "attend market and participate in trading" while "men sat at home and did the weaving."

But that was only a start. To be sure, the ancient Egyptians valorized male prowess and insisted that the primary role of women was to run the home and bear children. Nevertheless, in ancient paintings women are portrayed alongside men at every level of society, from coordinated ritual events to manual labor. In addition, all women, except slaves, enjoyed astonishing legal equality and financial independence. Women could own, buy, and sell property; they could borrow money, sign contracts, initiate divorce proceedings, and appear as witnesses in court. They could make wills and choose their beneficiaries. Records have been found indicating that women received equal pay for equal work. In such an environment, a poet like Hekenus might well have felt empowered to speak her mind and take charge of her life.

Hekenus's poem, inscribed on papyrus, is housed in the museum in Cairo. The papyrus is a bit bedraggled. It has many holes and frayed edges, and a number of areas have, over time, been rubbed out. I have used ellipses to indicate such lacunae and indeterminacies—one ellipsis representing a word or two, several ellipses representing a phrase or more. In a few cases, I have inserted brackets around a word or phrase because there seemed enough reason, to my mind, to conclude that the bracketed words or something akin to them were, in fact, what the poet intended.

Prosody represents a huge gap in our knowledge of ancient Egyptian poetry. Hieroglyphs had no vowels. Hence, though scholars have been able to understand and translate the language, they are unable to pronounce it. As a result they are also unable to scan the verse line. Does it rely on feet or duration? More than likely we will never know. Thus the prosodic constraints or approaches that may have existed played no part in the work of translation.

Form was another matter. As I have already noted, most ancient Egyptian poems were written in couplets. Fortunately, it was easy to ascertain where each of Hekenus's couplets began and ended because the first word in each couplet was written in red and a red dot marked its end.

The big surprises came with tone and content. Line by line, I realized I was working with a revolutionary document—a work with a point of view almost impossible to imagine before the women's liberation movement of the 1960s. Here was an ancient annunciation: Hekenus, exalted, chosen, it is unclear by whom, to be the virgin mother of a divine son—a son she is to conceive through the agency of Ka via the mouth. But, unlike the Virgin Mary, Hekenus will not submit to her "calling." She has a life to live, and live it she will. Surely, I had encountered the world's first outspoken feminist!

And then, the *coup de theatre:* Hekenus's mention of a people (presumably *her* people) "laid waste"—a reference that could be construed as confirmation of the text engraved on the stele of Merneptah discovered over a century ago and heretofore the only non-Biblical acknowledgment of the existence of Israel in relation to ancient Egypt.

"And This He Said" was destined to stand not only as a powerful and moving expression of a woman's emancipation, it was to become an important historical document as well. My first attempt at translation had borne stunning, unforgettable fruit!

Dish Rag

from the kitchen series

Oy,   Little tumult,

little racket.

My nudge, this nudnick heart.

Who wouldn't? What?   Worry?

Veys mir. that schmendrick!

That ganif! This

Schmootz

dragged in,   for what,

Genius?

The shmatttah not worth the needle;

that's what's mine to darn.   Feh!

And what is this? Everything

A little ongepatchka   though

who is there

but me   to set the daily lamps?

Still, thanks God.

There's schmoozing.

Here's a nosh

—a fish, a soup.

It's not nothing even in the dark

A shayna punim.   And the schvitzing?

I'm in a schvitz, thank you very much.

What's this?

     Bobkes. Utzing.

Nachas.

     Practically nothing and still the pupik shows.

Darling, my Bubala, the whole megillah.

                Amen.

TZADIE RACKEL (fl. early 19th c.)

TZADIE RACKEL is one of the Sewn Poets of the Jewish villages
and small cities of Bessarabia in the early 1800s. Unlike most
of her entirely anonymous sister poets, Tzadie Rackel actu-
ally stitched her name—though not her family name—into
each of her poems. For many years Tzadie Rackel's poems
were unknown. Even those who wore or owned
garments sewn by Tzadie did not necessarily find the poems
she'd included into her tailoring. It is believed that she is the
daughter of the tailor Tralinsky, from the small city of Reni
on the River Prut. The Tailor Tralinsky was known for his
fine craftsmanship and for having allowed his daughter to
refuse a marriage. Tzadie joined her father as a tailor. The
shop flourished under Tzadie's careful hand, and Reni briefly
became a textile destination known for fine embroidery and
clothworks. However, when the tailor died the shop closed,
since few trusted that a daughter could manage to carry on
the father's work and it was deemed improper for men to
have suits made by a woman. Eventually Tzadie was forced
into a door-to-door rag trade, going to wealthier Jewish
homes to sew and knit yearly necessities. A simple list of
these necessities—menstrual cloths, bed linens, trousseaus,
wedding dresses, mourning wear, drapes, socks, horse
blankets, aprons, rugs, as well as basic family garments—indi-
cate the range not only of Tzadie Rackel's sewing skills but
the opportunities she found for her subversive poetic art.

Considerations of Form

The known poems of Tzadie Rackel are poems to be handled. These poems are, in the deepest and most accurate sense, physical experiences. One speaks of the threading, stitching, the weaving, the fabric and texture in poetry—borrowing freely from tactile artisan crafts as a way to describe the unified effects of sound and sense, the formal arrangements in each poem. Here, however, to speak of the poem's surface texture demands an authentic regard of the poem's physical considerations. These are irrefutably poems in which form and content take on an additional formal dimension since all of the known poetry of Tzadie Rackel has been fabric-based, what we have come to identify as the stitched poem, the garment poem, or in certain discussions, the fabric poem.

If the poem is a made object then the surviving poems of Tzadie are truly poems to be worn (the slip, the coat, the apron poem series), sat upon (the slipcover series, the kilim pillows) or bedded and warmed under (the crocheted duvet cover, the appliqué linen sheet and pillow sets). There are poems to be walked across down lamp-lit hallways, as in the surviving but alas threadbare needlepoint rug poems. These poems complain, as in the dish-rag poems and diaper poems, but also there are deeply hopeful even instructive poems as in the bridal trousseau poems. There are poems of warning and provocation stitched on women's undergarments and across the woolen thigh bands of knit stockings.

If the effort Tzadie exerts reflects her dire artistic conditions (consider the many brilliant feminist considerations of generations of silenced women), it is clear the poet is well aware that the ultimate effect of her radical and outlaw method-ology is often coy, as when on the sole of a knitted sock the lines, "you poor schamaeel who inhales these words," are embroidered in petit-pointe.

On Translation and Yiddish

Translating Tzadie's poems has been challenging; I've encountered so many limitations. How, for example, to lineate a poem that in the original was sewn along the seams of a woman's slip? Could I find a way to bring to the page the particular bodies that wore Tzadie Rackel's poems? How to consider sonically the swell of a hip, the sag of a grandmother's once youthful breast? How shall the page embody the embodied poem? Since both figuratively and absolutely, these are poems that the original readers inhabited, I struggled to make an equivalent experience while not succumbing to cutesy or decorative ends. The household fabric poems also proved tricky to translate since the original poem relied on an active, working reader. Occasionally to find a line of Tzadie's poem one must smooth out the pleat of a drape. Tzadie often mended tablecloths with sewn poems. In these works old stains from a borscht or a Tzimmes becomes another and lived layer of the poem. No doubt a better translator would have conceived a better vehicle than the page for Tzadie Rackel's work.

Then, of course, there is the question of the Yiddish. Or, perhaps more specifically, how Yiddish, a dying language, has already been absorbed, less assimilated than obdurately, even stubbornly included and thus untranslatable into contemporary American English. One cannot underestimate Yiddish's absorption into the language.

But let me not shrug off my task as a translator so easily. Let me instead consider aloud some of the choices I encountered when attempting to translate Tzadie's poem. Let me start with the first of Tzadie's words in "Dish Rag": *Oy.* Can we consider *Oh,* which carries none of the disgust that burdens *Oy?* The vowel pressed against vowel sound closes off *Oy* without any of the opened-mouthed, back-throated possibilities of *Oh.* Again questions of form inform the choices to preserve or alter the Yiddish within the poem or to switch to a more normative English. For example the *Oy* that appears in a Tzadie Rackel's poems stitched into menstrual rags for a young woman might better be changed to *Oh,* and thus reflect a young woman's hopefulness and fear as she enters into womanhood.

Let me consider another moment in the poem that caused me great angst: the word *schmendrick,* which translates as fool. While fool was quickly eliminated for the jesterly ease of the word, I spent many drafts of this translation with *idiot* in place before I finally restored schmendrick to its position. When *schmendrick* is included in language, the felicitous presence of men can finally not be denied. If instead of *schmendrick* Tzadie had used the synonym *schlemiel*—I believe I would have gladly yielded to either *idiot* or *fool.*

It should be said that the poem included here is from the rag series of hand cloths. While there are finer, less embittered poems, this poem speaks, I think, painfully well to the difficulties that Tzadie faced. It should be noted that despite the poor cloth quality, the threads for the poem are silk, a wonderful and imaginative manifestation of Tzadie's lived conflict: to write her silken syllables on soiled dish cloths.

Thus I offer you this rag poem, inked on rag paper. I wish you could behold the multi-colored, multistitched fabrics of Tzadie Rackel, who made her art as any great artist does: syllable by stitch by hand by word by treadle.

The Movement of the Triangle

All human affairs are complicated

By what we know of the world's
Physical laws
                     & in *la dernière science de le coeur*

We must acknowledge that all specific
Gravity remains immense
No matter how adeptly the bed of the universe
Moves to accompany us

& surely it is those notations
Of music   poetry   & art   which remind us
Of our mortal attractions
                                 & so we seek

Constantly the harmony of the *three*
The triad   & some final   perfect chord

& it is the same in life

If we are the least bit honest about it
Just as every schoolboy knows that geometry

Is simply the logical & natural
Progression of

        propositions

& of course we know that the everlasting
Sentence of hell is each other
That is: the *three:*

              She   *He*   *They*

& because that sentence (to be diagrammed)
Contains no longer any verb not lost
To time
& because it is the fiction of every poem
That all lines will connect at some given point
Let me begin by drawing

The curtains open to the sky where
A grid of stars calmly

             punctuates the night

& slowly I will draw for you not one conclusion

Except to show that (however intimate
The essence of the *three*)
We must observe the movement of the triangle
In order to fully understand what we   what *they...*

Have truly lost

JEAN-PHILLIPE DARIENS (b. 1954-)

JEAN-PHILLIPE DARIENS was born in Nice on September 1, 1954. His mother, Anna Temoigne, was a well-known conceptual artist who moved with her son to Paris in the middle 1960s. His father, Paul Dariens, was a journalist who spent most of his career, until his death from leukemia in 1973, covering the shifting political climates of African nations. Though friendly, Jean-Phillipe's parents seem to have carried on a quite "casual" marriage, as he has referred to it in the one brief autobiographical prose piece he published in 1985.

In the late 1970s, Dariens fell in with the *Tel Quel* crowd and for a brief period worked as the assistant to the poet and editor Denis Roche at *Editions de Seuil*. He once said to me he thought of this as his true "coming of age" in the literary hot house of Paris during this heady period of critical and poetic revolution. Though he admired Roche and Marcelin Pleynet, another poet associated with *Tel Quel*, Jean-Phillipe's most resilient influences still seem to me to be Yves Bonnefoy and the lesser known but remarkable poet Jacques Réda.

As other poets of his generation continued to write themselves out of existence, towards an ever increasing belief in silence or the image as manifested in visual (not literary) culture, Dariens began to back away from this more theory-inflected work towards a more complex sense of poem, using a rich palette but a fiercer interior architecture in his work. Today, Jean-Phillipe Dariens divides his time between Paris, where he supports himself with journalism and freelance editing, and Prince Edward Island, Canada, at the family home of his wife Antoinette Dulage.

The Translation

The translation here is of an early poem of Jean-Phillipe Dariens' and it is also a poem that represents the very earliest period of our active (collaborative) tranlation of his work, dating from the spring of 1979.

I'd met Jean-Phillipe at the Hotel des Grandes Écoles, on the Rue du Cardinal Lemoine. He was staying in a ground-floor room in an annex building across from the main part of the hotel, a room that had clearly once been a kind of gardener's greenhouse or shed, as it was oddly shaped—a kind of imperfect triangle at the end of the annex—and had large opaque panes that made up the glass walls. The hotel had hung curtains across the walls of windows, but I remember that Jean-Phillipe would dramatically pull them open each morning so that the light would fill his small room. He'd been living at the hotel for nearly a year and had spent his first few months in an attic garret room (still the French tradition of where to put writers) until this more peculiar but wonderfully eccentric and gorgeous room had opened up. At that time he had no intention of leaving until he was thrown out, which he was the following summer (for not being able to pay his back rent).

It was there—in that glass-walled former shed—that we began translating his poems. Jean-Phillipe's English was far better than my French, and we stumbled along at first, but after some time I was able to get an increasingly more complicated sense of what he was after in his work—a kind of floating abstraction that he believed could be anchored with particular, even idiosynscratic, details and with at least some kind of oblique narrative line.

Looking back at this translation now after so many years, it occurs to me that I've been (both then and now, having tried to rework it a bit for this anthology) unable to capture the sense of shifting fluidity that Jean-Phillipe's poetry always has in French. My English, I'm afraid, makes it feel here—the poem's movement, I mean (and since the poem is all about movement this certainly is a dilemma)—a bit stultified and stiff, even wooden in places. Our later translations of Jean-Phillipe's poems strike me as being a bit more delicate and fluent in their movement, and I imagine the years of acquaintance and partnership in the translations have made that difference.

Since the mid-1990s Jean-Phillipe Dariens has written his poetry in a much more private atmosphere, absorbed professionally in the same politically inflected journalistic work that occupied his father for so many years. Just before his mother's death in 1997, Jean-Phillipe wrote the catalogue notes for her last significant gallery show, an impressive and highly moving retrospective of her life's work, including many photo documents of her more infamous and influential conceptual pieces. Most recently, in 2001, Jean-Phillipe published a book-length elegy simply entitled, "Anna Temoigne" in tribute and in memory of his mother. Twice in the past year he and I have discussed on the phone the possibility of renewing our collaboration in order to bring this work into English, but every time it seems we are about to embark on this project and look over the notes and versions I've assembled, Jean-Phillipe is suddenly off on assignment to some remote part of the world. It is my strong feeling that he has no real desire ever to see this poem in English, given the unusual intimacy of its details and bald passions, so unlike the more highly mathematical and elevated abstraction of his earlier work. Still, this elegy is—in my view—the clear apex of Dariens' career, and my hope is that he will finally relent and allow it to be brought into English.

From the Annals of Translation

A student of mine at the University of Chicago, Katia Mitova, came to my office not long ago with a problem. It was not the sort of problem students usually had— about a course or a late paper. It concerned some papers her mother had sent her.

Katia's mother lived in Sofia, in a large apartment house where there happened to live other women of her age who, like her, had been widowed, some as far back as the Second World War. These women avoided loneliness by maintaining close ties. Rarely would one be seen alone; they moved in groups to do the shopping, to walk in the park, or simply to sit in the sun. In the evening they would play cards or watch television. The oldest and most frail of them, Anna K., was seen less and less with the others, due to failing eyesight and limited hearing. It was generally thought that she had but a short while to live. One day she phoned Katia's mother and asked her to please come to see her.

Propped up in bed, Anna K. told Katia's mother that she wanted to give her something that she had had for years, but had not known what to do with. First, she said, she must tell her something of its history.

It seems that Anna had a half-brother. Her mother had been married briefly to a Russian engineer who, when he learned he was soon to be a father, returned to the Soviet Union just before his son Marin was born. Still in her early twenties and attractive, Anna's mother moved in with a promising young journalist who took care of her and her infant son. The arrangement was a happy one. Within a year they had Anna, and within two they moved into a spacious house. From the beginning Anna and her step-brother were close. Two years older than Anna, Marin was her mentor and protector, walking her to school, helping her with her homework, and telling her which boys she could befriend and which she shouldn't. He himself was an excellent student and during his teens wrote poems that were praised by his teachers and grudgingly admired by the other students. Anna recalled, however, that around the time he was sixteen things began to change. Marin would come home from school and instead of going out to spend time with his friends he would shut himself in his room. It was assumed that he was working on poems. His isolation from others, even from Anna, increased and seemed at times edgy and hostile. He continued to go to school, but made sure everyone knew that he did not want to be there. Finally, he announced to his parents that he was quitting. Naturally, they insisted that he continue and for days loud and bitter arguments took place. Then one night Anna, looking down from her window, saw Marin go behind the house and set fire to what she believed were the poems he had been writing. By morning Marin was gone. The note he left said only that he was going to join his "real" father in the Soviet Union. But in his haste to get away, he had forgotten to take a small notebook that he had hidden in the back of his closet and in which were written six highly contradictory, fanciful, and misleading autobiographical fragments.

Anna speculated that his journey must have been long and arduous, for it was only months later that they heard from his father that Marin had arrived. He had arrived but left very soon after. Conscripted into the Red Army, he was sent to the German front. It was there, during some of the most ferocious fighting of the war that he returned to poetry, writing his poems in a small notebook which he kept in his breast pocket. In February 1942, the young poet was killed by a German bullet that passed through his poems into his heart. His body was buried in a common grave, where it remains. The notebook, a crucifix, and some loose change were sent to Marin's father. Not knowing what to make of the notebook, he sent it to his ex-wife, who kept it in a box along with the six autobiographical fragments. Anna knew nothing of the box until her mother died and it was passed down to her along with other of her mother's possessions. There was no indication that her mother ever tried to read the poems, most of which were still stuck together with dried blood. Anna herself confessed that though she had tried to read the poems, she gave up after the first few. The hole, she said, was a problem. Finally, she passed Marin's poems and autobiographical writing on to Katia's mother, suspecting that Katia, who was known to be literary, would be their ultimate recipient. Katia, who had never heard of Marin, was delighted by the opportunity to "discover" the young poet's work. Her delight was short-lived, for it soon became depressingly clear that what she had been given were the sparse remains of a young man's inner life and that the zero left by the bullet not only memorialized his death, but more than likely cancelled the meaning of his poems.

Katia came to my office with her translations of the autobiographical fragments, which she found especially interesting. The poems, she said, would take more time. Her problem was that she felt responsible for the young poet's posthumous existence. Clearly, this was a responsibility she did not wish to bear alone. Would I look over what she had done and give her some advice as to how to proceed? Here are the fragments:

1. I was born on the side of a mountain in the depths of winter. My mother tells me that snow drifted to the second story and a tunnel had to be dug to open the front door. This was on February 3rd on the out skirts of Vratsa. I weighed nine and a half pounds at birth and was thought to have the makings of a giant. My height made people think I was at least a year older than I was. As a result, expectations for me were considerably greater than they were for others of my age.

2. While very young I wrote under an assumed name a prose masterpiece. It is not important, at least not to me, nor should it be to you, that this wonderfully precocious book is out of print. It is enough that I wrote it and must live with its memory, which casts a shadow over my many subsequent attempts to create works of value. The glory of that accomplishment was the grave of my hopes. The caused a sensation here in Bulgaria, and in France, Germany, and Finland as well. The only benefit I reaped was that of publicity. I became the most photographed fourteen-year-old in the history of Bulgarian literature. But that is not important. What is is that I turned my attention to poetry, and that has been my downfall.

3. We had been traveling for years to escape the dismal town of my birth, a small seaport with squat dark houses, each with a chimney from which smoke never ceased to rise, darkening its sky. We kept going no matter what the long-term advantages might have been of remaining in any particular place. We packed up our few belongings and hit the next town, staying in a cheap hotel or boarding house. What my father did

besides change jobs is a mystery. Whether he quit or was fired, I'll never know. My mother, when I would ask her, only shrugged her shoulders and sighed. My schooling was fragmented and inadequate, which, since it did not bother my parents, never bothered me. My father had an immense black beard that reached the top of his belly. My mother had long black hair that reached the small of her back. To say that they were an odd couple would be a mistake. They were perfectly matched.

4.   We lived in tents for a long time. My father liked the open air, sleeping on the ground, and going for days without washing. Personal hygiene was not a priority for either of my parents. Even my mother had a thick earthy smell about her. It goes without saying that I was a sickly child. We traveled by camel to places like Shiraz, Esfahan, Tabriz, Tehran, Baghdad, and Basra. My father was a trader, buying and selling rugs and trinkets. When I was eight years old my mother died, and I was sent to live with her sister in Sofia, where I went to school and did poorly. My father was killed by an American, who wanted a rug that my father would not sell him.

5.   I have spent my life trying to do away with my birth, but again and again the brute fact of it stymies me. Okay, you were born, I say to myself, but why not mark the beginning of your life when you first saw a tree or learned to call the sun the sun? Why only one beginning? Why not be a man of multiple births?

6.   When I was born the woman hanging laundry in the next yard burst into song and suddenly all the other women of Varna started to sing. Then they all stopped and there was silence. When I was born the men who stood on the beach staring at the sea turned around to face the hills behind them. The dogs at their side stood on their hind legs and bayed. Then they stopped and there was silence. What was it about my birth that elicited, with such magical suddenness, signs of approval followed by stony indifference? No wonder my birth has confused me and left me of two minds about the way I affect others.

What I noticed in these fragments was Marin's desire to locate himself anywhere but where he was born, and to find an alternative to a banality that he felt was imprisoning. They also displayed a sense of humor in relation to his parents, who were made to appear an unhappy mix of the exotic and the grotesque. Clearly he wished to locate himself in his writing, the only world over which he felt he had control.

As I read these fragments, I began to wonder what kind of poems Marin had written. I doubted that they would be what most of us think of as war poems, poems that register the horrors of battle, or that ruefully talk of the wounded or the dead, or that honor bravery. I suspected they would be more fanciful, maybe even surreal. The restlessness that I found in his prose might be characteristic of his poems. And then it occurred to me that the autobiographical fragments amounted to a cancellation of himself. They were a set of erasures that suggested a negative presence, that is, one that denies its own existence by fostering the notion that it is another. Hadn't he said in the fifth fragment, "I have spent my life trying to do away with my birth?"

I could not help but think of the horrible appropriateness of the bullet hole in the middle of his poems. If ever there were a negative presence that was it. Marin's death seemed designed just for him. In anticipating his poems, I began to think less of what they might be and more about the zero at their center. I even thought that what surrounded the zero might prove to be irrelevant, that the true poem resided in the zero itself.

Did a zero need translating? And if the zero was the dominant feature of the poems, did it matter what surrounded it? A line from an early poem of mine suddenly came to me, "Wherever I am I am what is missing." No wonder it was so easy for me to base the value of Marin's poems—although I had not yet read them—on the part of them that was missing. I had an intuitive grasp of what was not there. No, the zero did not need translating. But if I were to fill the zero with what I felt the bullet had taken away, would that be translating or would it be rewriting? It would certainly change what I had chosen to believe was the central character of the poems-what gave them, for me, their tragic dimension. In other words, it would normalize them, make them seem like other poems, and would force them to be judged without consideration for the very thing that set them apart. It might also be a kind of falsification. That is, if what existed before the zero was written in Bulgarian, how could I supply the missing original in English? I would be inventing and not translating. Besides, as a translator, I did not believe in taking liberties. But if I were to translate from a language I did not know, could it be said that I was taking liberties? Can one translate from a language he does not know? Some claim to, but they are actually editing someone else's literal version. Since I had no desire to put something where the zero was, such considerations were purely academic. It was my duty to preserve the zero, even without knowing what the rest of these poems might be. I believed in its modest and fateful emptiness. How could I improve on what was so clearly and indivisibly itself! So powerful was my attraction to the zero of Marin's poems that I playfully considered erasing the part of them that was written, thus extending the zero and creating invisible poems. There was no precedent for such a tactic because of course no survivors exist. I was so charmed by this notion that I almost called Katia to tell her that we could dispense with her having to translate the written remains of Marin's poems. But it became clear that such a plan would erase rather than extend the zero. The zero needed a shaping circumference. That is, it had to mean nothing rather than be nothing. To invoke Wallace Stevens for a moment, it was a case of having the nothing that is there instead of the nothing that is not there.

Then I began to wonder what it would do to the zero if the surrounding poem was bad or just unexceptional. Would the clarity, precision, and beauty of the zero be damaged? If what Marin had written was not good, would it be wrong to make what I believed to be poem-saving changes? Probably. But then again, would not a good poem surrounding the zero make the presence of the zero that much more moving? And yet, what could I possibly write that would do justice to it? Nothing came to mind. The influence of the zero was overwhelming.

To rid myself of this excessive valuation of the zero, I decided I would have to fill it in. At first, I thought that I'd have to see what remained of Marin's poems. Then I thought it might be more interesting if I just wrote a series of short round poems that would fit in the middle of his poems. All I would need were the measurements of the hole. Somehow, however, I was reluctant to call Katia to tell her of my plan. She would almost certainly be shocked. My plan, I felt sure she would say, was nothing more than undermining of the solemn reminder of Marin's death. After all, it was the hole that made his poems so irrefutably personal. Of course, I could write little round poems and dispense with Marin's surrounding words. Then I could extend what began as round poems to poems of a rectangular shape. In other words, I could fill in the hole and write poems that would eradicate whatever existed of the originals. Not a nice thing to do. And my only justification would be that my poetry was better than his. This was debatable, since I had not as yet laid eyes on Marin's poems.

Nor had I considered the possibility that Marin's poems would be very good, too good to be translated by Katia, too good to be played with by me. Perhaps my fascination with what was missing in Marin's poems and making that what I felt should be retained, was only an unconscious way of acknowledging that something was missing from my own work, something central around which hovered the words I had managed to write, the things I had managed to say. But why would I elevate that which I had failed to accomplish? No, such a reading did not make sense. That is, the zero for me had become a mirror, a mirror in which I saw nothing. Where my features had been I saw a void, an openness, infinite and unanalyzable. Marin was my double. His absence was my absence. "Wherever I am I am what is missing." That line was the message of Marin's poems, but I had written it years before I knew of them.

I called Katia and told her that I'd like to see the poems when what I really wanted to see was the hole. When she brought me the poems, which she had separated from the spiral binder, I was struck by their frailty. I held one up to the window, then held it against the white wall of my living room. I kept looking at it, holding it up, then down. I brought it close to my eye and looked through to the world outside. A car came by. A gust of wind shook a few leaves down from the trees. A few crows crossed my line of vision.

Insomnia, Bastard Child

of space and time, I welcome
all your unannounced visits,
the sugar cube of darkness
you leave on my tongue,

those cracks in the walls
where loneliness finds beauty.
Because of you I get first dibs
on the boots the moon laces up

to hurdle planets. Spiders write
bad checks across the ceiling.
Fat windows snore. Insomnia,
champagne and sleep are overrated,

no match for your set design
and stage props. Please stick around
until dawn. Otherwise, I'll wake
to gaze into a puddle of drool

only to find I am still myself, just
another bland fact, neither sweet

nor dark, lonely or beautiful.
And what's the use of remembering

the obvious, of gratuitous dreams
that filch what you, bastard child, alone
can bestow—the lipstick abandoned
on the glass, the moth on its way to fire.

Slaaploosheid, Bastaard Kind

van ruimte en tijd, ik welkom
je onverwacht bezoek,
het suikerklontje van donkerheid
die je op mijn tong laat,

die spleten in muren waar
eenzaamheid schoonheid vindt.
Vanwege jou heb ik de eerste beet
aan de laarsen die de maan aantrekt

om over planeten te springen. Spinnekoppen
krabben slechte cheques op 't plafond.
Vette vensters snurken. Slaaploosheid,
champagne en slaap zijn niets waard

in vergelijking met je regie
en toneelversiering. Blijf toch nog wat,
tot dageraad. Anders wordt ik wakker
in een kwijlenpoel, om uit te vinden

dat ik nog altijd mezelf ben, gewoon
maar een flauw gegeven, nog zoet
of donker, eenzaam of mooi.
Waartoe dient het zich aan het duidelijke

te herinneren, de kostelooze dromen
die stelen wat jij alleen kan schenken,
jij bastaard kind - verlaten lippenstift
op het glas, een nachtvlinder opweg naar vlam.

Jan DeKeerk (b. 1939)

PLODDING AND DELIBERATE, Jan DeKeerk's poetic output over the last four decades has been relatively small, considering that his first book, *These Fingers Are Made of Rum*, was originally published in Flemish in 1966. This collection was later translated into English by Dr. Arnold P. Schnagel, the distinguished Columbia University scholar and leading authority on contemporary Flemish writers.

For five years DeKeerk traveled through India and Asia with his wife, Madeleine Weets. The couple subsequently returned to Belgium and purchased a small farm near Verlijnde, the rural village north of Ghent where as a child DeKeerk had been raised by his grandparents. He published three slim but celebrated poetry collections between 1974 and 1995—*Gasket, Nozzle, Hoist; What If We Cannot Trust It;* and *Syncopation.* The latter book is a series of poems exploring the convergences between language and notable jazz riffs from American composers such as Gershwin, Ellington, Gillespie, Evans, Monk and Coltrane. A longtime amateur jazz clarinetist, DeKeerk has shunned public performance. "My most enduring audience," he recently confessed in a newspaper interview, "continues to be the birds and rodents who take up residence on our farm."

In 2002, DeKeerk was awarded one of Belgium's most prestigious literary honors, Koninklijke Prijs voor Hedendaagse Vlaamse Poëzie, for *Polders: New and Selected Poems.* "Insomnia, Bastard Child" was a new poem in that collection.

Though born in the month the Nazis invaded Poland, and World War II officially commenced, Jan DeKeerk has never been an overtly political poet. His poems are propelled by the playful and the unruly, tempered by a touch of the absurd. And he has always enjoyed squeezing the mundane and the familiar through the needle-eyes of sharp, and sometimes whimsical, philosophical perspectives. That said, in the only essay on poetry and poetics DeKeerk has ever written—"Even the Dream Is Dreaming"—he argues, "the lyric poem is the most viable weapon humanity has ever forged to fight tyrants and despots, to overwhelm those who would oppress, enslave and terrorize others."

Smoke and Bourbon: A Glimpse at the Poetry of Jan DeKeerk

To read the small yet capacious poems of Jan DeKeerk is to metabolize the Aristotelian idea that poetry should delight as it instructs. A master of the understated entrance, DeKeerk creates narratives wherby the reader feels both distressed and comforted. In his poems, something or someone is always at risk. Such urgencies may be playful, ironic or deadly serious or some combination of all three. But they are always present.

Not surprisingly, DeKeerk's personas are protean, unpredictable. They whisper and boast, seduce and lament, guffaw and cajole, pound their fists and cry out. They show us how people and ideas that bring relief can also bring danger—the linguistic equivalent of Robert Duvall's lurking-in-the-shadows-behind -the-bedroom-door portrayal of Boo Radley in the film version of *To Kill A Mockingbird*. If insomnia, that rambunctious, illegitimate kid, arrives unannounced to disrupt any possibility of sleep, at least he brings with him those places in the walls "where loneliness finds beauty."

Concurrently, DeKeerk's supple and acrobatic language begs to be spoken aloud, gobbled up by teeth and tongue. Despite living in a climate where flora flourish, Belgians don't bring flowers to parties. They bring chocolate or licorice. They love their salted or sweet licorice, and argue their chocolate is far superior to Swiss chocolate, because cognac or rum is one of the key ingredients. Belgian chocolate is, literally, intoxicating.

DeKeerk's poems are pure mouth-candy. "Insomnia, Bastard Child" is no exception. *"Het suikerklontje van donkerheid / die je op mijn tong laat,"*— chewy syllables Dr. Schnagel aptly translates as "the sugar cube of darkness / you leave on my tongue." In the poem's fifth stanza, a delicious continuum of o's provides zip—*"nog zoet / of donker, eenzaam of mooi"* ("neither sweet /nor dark, lonely or beautiful").

The poem's final maneuver is driven by succulent monosyllabic words and sweeping v and l sounds: *"verlaten lippenstift / op het glas, een nachtvlinder opweg naar vlam."* Schnagel's adroit translation captures the music and propulsion of DeKeerk's Flemish while preserving the integrity of the epiphanic double clauses. "The lipstick abandoned / on the glass, the moth on its way to fire." And let's not forget that DeKeerk's mouth-candy is calorie-free. In this age of mad diets and stomach staples, what more could we ask?

* * * * *

Alto saxophonist Charlie Parker called the notes he so furiously and astonishingly played beneath, behind and above the melody, "figures." Bird hopped from musical idea to idea, creating spontaneous phrasings and harmonic complexities. In similar fashion, DeKeerk often establishes a central riff or phrase and then effortlessly improvises subsequent moves. He delights in cranking out trochaic lines and syncopated beats. "Spiders write / bad checks across the ceiling. / Fat windows snore." Yes they do, as his tones snap, pop and reverberate.

He also knows that such clipped rhythms can become monotonous. But not if the poet alters the cadence. And so DeKeerk follows the aforementioned lines with the adagio plea, "Insomnia, / champagne and sleep are overrated, / no match for your set design / and stage props."

And from saxophonists Dexter Gordon and Sonny Rollins (those wonderful bastard virtuoso children of Parker and Lester Young) DeKeerk has learned how each phrase is strengthened by the notes not played, the ideas not said. Long after we've set aside a DeKeerk poem, the silences resonate. Schnagel agrees. He asserts that this wood-shedding clarinetist's poems are smoke and bourbon, create their own bebop vocabularies. "When we read DeKeerk's poems," Schnagel writes, "we feel as if we've been offered a front-row seat in our favorite tiny nightclub."

DeKeerk has never been one to align himself with any poetic "school" or tradition; however, if we study his entire body of work we can draw one substantial conclusion. He is not interested in presenting big, complicated words, but in imaginatively delivering big, complicated ideas through small, crisp words.

DeKeerk's poems have never imitated life. They anticipate life. And in that anticipation they help us generate more meaningful questions about the possibilities of human existence. "What's the use of remembering / the obvious…" is not only a caution to the psyche but an *ars poetica.* If nothing else, the poet's task, poem after poem, is to create language that unexpectedly twists, thwarts, upends and satisfies the reader's expectations. After all, in the jazzy universe of Jan DeKeerk, we get dibs on the boots the moon laces up to hurdle planets.

From the Notebooks of Anne Verveine, VI

You are dead, therefore I write to you.
I am dead, therefore I write to you.
Did we ever kiss? The shadow airplane

swooped down to smack the tarmac silently.
That crash didn't crash. The kiss
did but dissipated

in air like phantom smoke
rising from my shadow chimney inching
its way all afternoon across

the neighbors' slanted roof-
heat gusts escaping up the flue and printing themselves
as visible ghosts trailing

off to a chilly Empyrean.
February gleams on the roof slates.
As if the fire were real. As if

the heart pumped real blood.

ANNE VERVEINE (1965-?)

ANNE VERVEINE was born in 1965 in the village of Magagnosc, just outside the town of Grasse in the region of the south of France known as the Midi. The Alps plunge down to the Mediterranean here, and the *département* is called, logically enough, the Alpes-Maritimes. Grasse clings to the slope with steep, zigzagging streets and stone stairways, some of them medieval. From its narrow parks rise palm trees, mimosas, eucalyptus, umbrella pines; with its terracotta roof tiles and ochre stucco walls, the town feels more Italian than French. Grasse is famous for its perfumeries, and for being the birthplace of the 18th-century painter of aristocratic, pastoral frivolities, Jean-Honoré Fragonard. Verveine attended the *lycée* in Grasse, taking the bus five kilometers each day from Magagnosc where she lived with her parents and older sister over the family's modest photography shop. Any account of Verveine must steep itself in this ancient, sun-smitten landscape with its scents of lavender and thyme and its medieval masonry: even Magagnosc, darkly crammed on a spur of rock thrusting out from the slope, has its little Romanesque church.

Verveine is an elusive presence—one might even say absence—in contemporary French letters. She completed her studies in the classical curriculum in the *lyçée*, concentrating in Latin and philosophy, and passed her *baccalauréat* with high marks. There her formal education halted. She worked for several years in the family shop before moving to Paris, where she lived in a *chambre de bonne* on the Rue de Lille in the 7th *arrondissement,* and eventually found work as a graphic designer and lay-out artist for a small publisher of art books. She lived reclusively in the capital, publishing a few poems in small provincial journals, and hardly frequenting "literary society." Her friends seem to have been artists, photographers, and designers.

From her poems and notebook entries, and from the few accounts of herself she confided to her sister Eliane, we may assume that aside from the daily practice of writing poems and her work in the visual arts, the most significant event in Verveine's life was her encounter with one man, the exiled painter from Uzbekistan whom she met in Paris. For roughly five years, from 1985 to 1990, she lived in close, even passionate contact with this man whose name remains a mystery. Perhaps because of the break-up of the Soviet Union, he returned to Uzbekistan in 1990, and there is no evidence of further communication between him and Verveine after that point. In January of 2000, Verveine informed her family that she was travelling to Uzbekistan. They received letters from her from Tashkent, Samarkand, and Bukhara. In March the letters ceased. By July, the family began attempting, fruitlessly, to track her down with the aid of the French consulate in Uzbekistan. Anne Verveine was last seen hitchhiking west of Bukhara near the border of Turkmenistan in August 2000. She is presumed kidnapped or dead.

The Poetry of Anne Verveine

She cuts an odd figure in late 20th, early 21st century French poetry. There is little to go on: only twenty-odd poems appeared in print in small provincial journals in what we can assume to have been her lifetime. She has little in common with her French contemporaries and immediate elders; she is less philosophical than Bonnefoy, less aphoristic than Char, less abstract than Royet-Journoud and Anne-Marie Albiach. Yet in her abrupt economies, her non sequiturs, the dream-like associative logic of her images, Verveine is certainly a child of modernity, and of French modernity at that.

She writes a fluid free verse, clustering in couplets and tercets. Hers is a cadenced freedom; one overhears, here and there in her lines, traditional French octosyllabic and decasyllabic verses, and occasionally an alexandrine bearing witness to her inheritance. Her lines do not rhyme. Even in their reliance on dramatically staged syntax for their expressive effects, however, they have a kind of bodily fullness in their assonances and alliterations. As a translator, I have striven to preserve her rhythmical character by threading traditional English cadences into the free verse fabric, as in the several pentameters in "From the Notebooks of Anne Verveine, VI": "swooped down to smack the tarmac silently." I have tried as well to present some version of her phonetic effects; "smack" and "tarmac," for instance, pick up the reverberations of the French "claquer" and "macadam." One cannot always be so direct, however; in most cases, one adapts and shifts these events in sound, hoping not for one-to-one correspondences, but for an analogous acoustic texture over-all.

Verveine's sources are clearly various. With her penchant for building poems around half-suppressed anecdotes, she sets up brutal little dramas that align her work more with 19th century French poetry than with her own time: "…You/ stood over me as I woke, I opened my eyes, I saw/ that I'd seen and that it was too/ late…" (from Poem I). However oblique, she remains a storyteller, a dramatist; a poet of direct address, and of objects, place, and incident. Her sources lie farther afield than France alone. The delicate ear will pick up echoes of the Latin poems of Catullus, Horace, Ovid and Virgil she studied in the lycée and apparently continued to read during her years in Paris. Poem V, for instance, lifts a line and a half right out of Virgil's First Eclogue. "You moved slowly, in shadow, teaching the shadows/ to echo my name" recasts Virgil's shadowy music: "Tu, Tityre, lentus in umbra/ formosam resonare doces Amaryllida silvas" (You, Tityrus, teach the woods to resound with the name of beautiful Amaryllis). It is characteristic of Verveine to treat her stolen goods with ferocity: the gentle eroticism latent in Virgil is startled into action in Verveine's next line: "You ripped my shirt at the neck."

The Latin poets haunt Verveine in verbal echoes. In setting and in her use of mythology as a language of experience, as well, she reminds us of the Latinate character of her native land, the South of France, once so thoroughly colonized by the Romans. The myth of Actaeon, a Greek tale made Roman by Ovid, structures Verveine's Poem I, and the fountain in Poem II with its garden deities ("three nymphs with moss staining their haunches, a pug-nosed faun") declares a continuity between Verveine's classicism and the fountains of her childhood village and its neighboring town, Grasse. But this young woman was a reader of the Psalms as well as of the classics. When she quotes Psalm 22 ("I am poured out like water") in her Poem VII in its meditation on eros, we see her once again wrenching a source out of its context for her own purposes. Similarly, in her adaptations from the Persian of Hafiz, in Poem IV, she plunders the amorous, mystical Sufi tradition for her own experience of ecstasy and loss.

It remains to be said that Anne Verveine's poems define a fairly narrow range of experience. In fact, the conventional femininity of their inspiration is almost an embarrassment. The poems excavated from the notebooks she left behind in Paris form one erotic sequence, and derive all their energy from the encounters of a feminine "I" with a male "you." These encounters are all the more charged for being envisioned through absence and distance. The lost lover, the painter in fire who opened Verveine's eyes to Persian poetry and textile art and the lure of the Silk Road, stepped out of his own lost world to introduce Verveine to passion, to distance, to suffering, and to song, almost simultaneously. In so doing, he moved her to invent her own kind of pastoral poem: as sad as Virgil's, and in its transient felicity, as fragile.

Pandora Novak

I have been tired of late, the old trunk with the rusted lock
stays closed most days, but now and then, I lift the lid
again; it's where I keep the few things that I care to keep—

a book of myths half-eaten by the moths, my mother's sable
brushes, dried tubes of oil paint, a fur-lined cape I wore
that winter we toured Russia, and the formal gown

of taffeta—a shocking green I wore to sing the part of Eve
in the opera called *Paradis*, by a composer long since dead
and never very good; its *mise-en-scène* was pastoral—

a grove of painted trees hung with fat, gilded fruit,
where large-eyed lions, fox and deer cuddled up together—
Edenic stage from which predation had been banned.

Oh that was sweet, with all its melodies of peace, and me
entranced, engaged to a tenor in a light buff body-suit;
our duet lavishly praised in the Paris press (which got us

the Russian tour).The bass was a tall man, who lounged
against the tree whose fruit I was forbidden—and after him,
the tenor seemed a bore, and Eden just a cardboard set,

and whoring for applause seemed all at once a trap
in which I'd stepped, its iron claws catching the fabric
of the dream that brought me there. I threw my clothes

into the trunk, half-empty now, once filled with the tools
of my father's cast-off trade: a make-up kit, a colorful
array of silken scarves and magic tricks, a rabbit

stuffed, whose glass eyes caught the light until it seemed
the very life; a deck of cards, a set of silver rings, a box
with hidden springs permitting an escape. I have been

travelling ever since.The tall bass left me somewhere
in the Alps, or I left him—I can't recall. But the snow
had begun to melt in the mountains, the air was clear

and I could breathe at last; I felt as new as a snake
must feel who's shed her skin and left it, a dry husk
for the wind to fondle. I've learned to travel light,

and leave no footprints in the snow. But still, I keep
this trunk—its magic made my father's way, and mine,
since I was the girl he sawed in half—

and while the crowd cheered and he took his bows,
I got away. I've left his tricks behind, but kept these shreds
of the life I fled when I chanced to look inside.

IRENA ZUPANIK (b. ca. 1870)

IRENA ZUPANIK was primarily known as "La Duchesse," a French sobriquet (a double entendre referring both to an aristocratic manner and a luscious autumn variety of pear) which she acquired during her years on the musical stage, where she was known for the purity of her soprano voice, the lush sensuality of her abundant physical presence, and as a latter-day proponent of Libertinage, the 17th-century philosophy of Pierre Gassendi which attempted to reconcile Epicureanism with Christianity. Though certainly Eastern European by descent, her exact nationality is unknown, for her theatre family cloaked its origins in a glamorous veil of mystery.

Her father was the famous magician and con man, Drago Zupanik, immortalized in the 19th-century Slovenian picaresque novel, *Drago ni doma (Drago Is Not at Home);* he traveled Europe, always just a little ahead of the law, performing with little Irena as his stage assistant and shill from the time she was eight or ten years old. She was probably born around 1870; she lived in Paris during the years of her operatic acclaim, where she was at the center of the rather infamous *Salon Impudique,* a kind of *demi-monde* collection of radicals, *literati,* artists and theatre people. Within a decade of her coming to prominence as an actress and singer, she suddenly disappeared from the stage and the public eye, and nothing more is known of her life after 1900. It was rumored that she was also a writer, though it was only in the mid-1990s that, quite by chance, a manuscript of her poems came to light.

A FRENCH LITERARY THEORIST of my acquaintance had purchased an old trunk in an antique shop in Ljubljana, and found in it a collection of Irena Zupanik's poems, written in French, though clearly ignorant of or indifferent to the poetry of Rimbaud and Mallarmé and their followers. Or it may have been that her avoidance of the symbolist mode came of its claims to the poet's role as magician, a role to which her own history may have given her an aversion. In any case, the theorist (whose name I omit out of fear of professional reprisals) pronounced the poems "a mere curiosity, revealing a tawdry sensibility and a female propensity to mirror-gazing." It was his contempt that first sparked my interest in the collection; entitled *Fauxtobiographie,* its name and strategy were clearly meant to disclaim any personal reading of its content, each pseudo-confession taking the voice of a different persona, poems which together struck me by their declaration of vagrancy, their bawdy elegance, their easy-going irreverence.

In the poem I have selected to translate for this anthology, Zupanik adopts the persona of a modernized Pandora, a choice which allows her to take possession of a much-maligned mythic character, one who—like the Eve her persona plays in the poem's opera—becomes not the creation and victim of a tyrant god's entrapment *(don't open that! don't eat that!)* but an independent agent. Zupanik's poem of mock-confession, given the time of its composition, was perhaps a playful but pointed comment on the way in which women's writing was mainly confined to the private sphere and its forms—diaries and letters in the main, while condemned in public to the realm of silence. Her Pandora appealed to me for a somewhat different reason: its use of the persona reinforced my own sense that an absolute degree of difference between the writer and the speaker is best for poetry, the distance conferring imaginative freedom, an escape from the over-examined life, the personal confession of the already known, which has claimed so much of the literature of the last half of the 20th century in America.

Zubanik's poem, though written in French, owes much to a traditional and strict Eastern European formalism, whose elaborate patterns she handles with a deceptive naturalness, a combination all but impossible to render in modern English. Thus I have employed the unrhymed triplet form to suggest at least the ghost of that prescribed but artfully hidden form, and have done my best to shift a late 19th–century pan-European voice into our own idiom, with what success I leave the reader to judge.

Contributors Biographies

Aliki Barnstone's most recent books of poems are *Blue Earth* (Iris Press, 2004) and *Wild With It* (Sheep Meadow Press, 2002). Two books are forthcoming: her translation, *The Collected Poems of C.P Cavafy* (Norton), and her study, *Changing Rapture: Emily Dickinson's Poetic Development* (University Press of New England). In 2005-2006 she will in reality be in Greece, where she hopes for a long imaginary conversation with her heteronym, Eva Victoria Perera, and that the full volume, *Eva's Voice,* will emerge.

Josh Bell's first book is *No Planets Strike,* (Zoo Press, 2005). He is a PhD candidate at the University of Cincinnati.

Laure-Anne Bosselaar is the author of *The Hour Between Dog and Wolf* and of *Small Gods of Grief,* winner of the *Isabella Gardner Prize for Poetry* for 2001. Her fourth anthology *Never Before: Poems About First Experiences,* will be published by Four Way Books in the fall of 2005. She teaches a graduate poetry workshop at Sarah Lawrence College.

Martha Collins' book-length poem *Blue Front* will be published by Graywolf in 2006; she is also the author of four collections of poems, most recently *Some Things Words Can Do,* and a chapbook, *Gone So Far* (Barnwood, 2005). She has co-translated two collections of poetry from the Vietnamese, most recently *Green Rice* by Lam Thi My Da (Curbstone, 2005, with Thuy Dinh), and teaches at Oberlin College, where she is Pauline Delaney Professor of Creative Writing.

Annie Finch's books of poetry include *Calendars* (Tupelo, 2003), *Eve* (Story Line, 1997), *The Encyclopedia of Scotland* (Salt, 2004); and a translation of the complete poetry of Louise Labé (Chicago, 2005). Her new collection of essays, *The Body of Poetry: Essays on Women, Form, and the Poetic Self,* is published in the Poets on Poetry Series from the University of Michigan Press (2005). She is Director of the Stonecoast low-residency MFA in creative writing at the University of Southern Maine.

Judith Hall is the author of three books of poetry, most recently *The Promised Folly* (TriQuarterly Books, 2003). She teaches at the California Institute of Technology and with the graduate writing program at New England College; she also serves as poetry editor of *The Antioch Review.*

Barbara Hamby is the author of three books of poems—*Delirium* (U. of North Texas, 1995), *The Alphabet of Desire* (NYU Press, 1999) and *Babel* (U. of Pittsburgh Press, 2004). She teaches in the Creative Writing Program at Florida State University.

Jennifer Michael Hecht's new book, *Funny,* won the University of Wisconsin Press 2005 Felix Pollak Poetry Prize. Her *Next Ancient World* (Tupelo, 2001) won the Poetry Society of America's 2002 Norma Farber First Book Award. Hecht is the author of *Doubt: A History* (HarperCollins, 2004) and *The End of the Soul* (Columbia University, 2003) which won the Phi Beta Kappa Society's 2004 Ralph Waldo Emerson Award. Her verse and reviews appear in *Poetry, Ms. Magazine, The Best American Poetry 1999* and 2006 (Scribners), *The New York Times* and *The American Scholar.*

Garrett Hongo is the author of *Volcano: A Memoir of Hawai`i* (Vintage, 1996). He is Distinguished Professor of Arts and Sciences at the University of Oregon

Andrew Hudgins teaches in the writing program at Ohio State University. He is the author of six books of poetry, the most recent being *Ecstatic in the Poison* (Overlak, 2003) and *Babylon in a Jar* (Mariner, 1998). In 2004-05 he was awarded a Guggenheim Fellowship.

David Kirby is the Robert O. Lawton Distinguished Professor of English at Florida State University and the author most recently of *The Ha-Ha* and *I Think I Am Going To Call My Wife Paraguay: Selected Early Poems.* For more information, see www.davidkirby.com.

Maxine Kumin's fifteenth book, *Jack and Other New Poems,* was published in 2005. The recipient of a Pulitzer, a Ruth E. Lilly, and a Poets' Prize, she was awarded Harvard's Medal for the Arts in May, 2005. She and her husband live on a farm in New Hampshire.

Khaled Mattawa is the author of two books of poems, *Zodiac of Echoes (Ausable, 2003)*, and *Ismailia Eclipse (Sheep Meadow, 1995)* He has translated five volumes of contemporary Arabic poetry and co-edited two anthologies of Arab American literature. He's been awarded the Alfred Hodder Fellowship from Princeton University, a Guggenheim fellowship, the PEN American Center Poetry in Translation Prize, and two Pushcart prizes. He teaches creative writing at the University of Michigan, Ann Arbor.

D. A. Powell's most recent book is *Cocktails* (Graywolf, 2004). He teaches at The University of San Francisco.

Kevin Prufer is the author, most recently, of *Fallen from a Chariot* (Carnegie Mellon, 2005) and *The Finger Bone* (Carnegie Mellon, 2002). He is also editor of *The New Young American Poets* (Southern Illinois, 2000), *Dark Horses: Essays On Overlooked Poems* (University of Illinois, 2005, with Joy Katz) and *Pleiades: A Journal of New Writing.* He lives in rural Missouri.

Anna Rabinowitz's volumes of poetry include *Darkling,* (Tupelo Press, 2001), a book-length acrostic poem now being developed into an experimental music theatre work by American Opera Projects, and *At The Site of Inside Out* (University of Massachusetts Press, 1997). *The Wanton Sublime* is due from Tupelo Press in Spring 2006. Among her awards are a National Endowment for the Arts Fellowship and the Juniper Prize. She is publisher and executive editor of *American Letters & Commentary.*

Victoria Redel is the author of 2 poetry collections and 2 books of fiction. Her novel, *Loverboy,* (Harvest 2002*)* was awarded the S. Mariela Gable Novel Award, The Foreward Fiction Award, Borders Original Voices and was a 2001 *LA Times* Best Books. It has recently been adapted for a film directed by Kevin Bacon. *Swoon,* (University of Chicago, 2003) her most recent collection of poems, was a finalist for the Laughlin Poetry Prize. She is on the faculty at Sarah Lawrence College and the Graduate Writing Program at Columbia University.

David St. John is the author of nine collections of poetry, most recently *The Face: A Novella in Verse* (HarperCollins, 2004). He is the Director of the Ph. D. Program in Literature and Creative Writing at The University of Southern California and lives in Venice Beach.

Mark Strand is the author of ten books of poems, including *Blizzard of One* (Knopf, 1998), which won the Pulitzer Prize. He has also published two books of prose and several volumes of translations. His honors include the Bollingen Prize, three grants from the National Endowment for the Arts, a Rockefeller Foundation award, and fellowships from The Academy of American Poets, the MacArthur Foundation, and the Ingram Merrill Foundation. He has served as Poet Laureate of the United States and currently teaches in the Committee on Social Thought at the University of Chicago.

Thom Ward is Editor at BOA Editions, Ltd. His poetry collections include *Small Boat with Oars of Different Size* (Carnegie Mellon, 1999), *Various Orbits* (Carnegie Mellon, 2003) and *Tumblekid* (University of South Carolina-Aiken).

Rosanna Warren teaches Comparative Literature at Boston University. Her most recent book of poems is *Departure* (Norton, 2003).

Eleanor Wilner bears some resemblance to the poet she translated: the green dress, the uncertain ancestry, the phototropism (especially to lighted exit signs). And like Irena she writes poetry; her newest book is *The Girl With Bees In Her Hair* (Copper Canyon Press, 2004).